**Everyman's Poetry**

*Everyman, I will go with thee,*
*and be thy guide*

# Alexander Pope

Selected and edited by DOUGLAS BROOKS-DAVIES

**EVERYMAN**
J. M. Dent • London

Introduction and other critical apparatus
© J. M. Dent 1996

J. M. Dent
Orion Publishing Group
Orion House
5 Upper St Martin's Lane
London WC2H 9EA

Typeset by Deltatype Ltd, Ellesmere Port, Cheshire
Printed in Great Britain by
The Guernsey Press Co. Ltd, Guernsey, C.I.

British Library Cataloguing-in-Publication
Data is available upon request.

ISBN 0 460 87798 4

# Contents

In loving memory of my mother, Peggy,
*matrum optima*
23 November 1913–12 January 1996

# Note on the Author and Editor

ALEXANDER POPE was born into a Catholic family in 1688, a few months before the 'Glorious Revolution' which saw the expulsion of Catholic James II and the accession of Protestant William III. Denied a formal grammar or public school education because of his religion, Pope nevertheless became intimately acquainted with ancient Greek and Roman literature while writing verse himself, and in his late teens became part of the London literary world. With Jonathan Swift, John Gay and others he founded the Scriblerus Club (devoted to exposing pedantry and ignorance while jestingly displaying its members' own brilliance, it would eventually lead to Pope's *Dunciad* and Swift's *Gulliver's Travels*). Publishing regularly from 1711 (*Essay on Criticism*), he moved quickly to his translation of the *Iliad*, while developing an increasingly satirical voice against Whig politics and the money culture that (as he saw it) attended it. Lampooned and attacked for his physical deformity (caused by tuberculosis of the bone) and his suspected Jacobitism, Pope became the main satirical poet of his generation, lambasting folly and upholding the values of rationality and decorum in all aspects of life. His Horatian poems testify to him as a man of many friendships, but it is the *Dunciad* that remains his main and most outrageously splendid achievement.

DOUGLAS BROOKS-DAVIES was born in London and educated at Merchant Taylors' School, Crosby and Brasenose College, Oxford. Formerly Senior Lecturer in English Literature at the University of Manchester, and currently Honorary Research Fellow in English there, he is now a freelance scholar. He has published widely on post-1550 English literature, his main contributions on the eighteenth century being on Fielding, Defoe and Pope (*The Mercurian Monarch*, 1983; *Pope's 'Dunciad' and the Queen of Night*, 1985).

# Chronology of Pope's Life

| Year | Age | Life |
| --- | --- | --- |
| 1688 | | 21 May, born in London to Edith and Alexander |
| c. 1697 | 9 | At school at Twyford, near Winchester |
| c. 1698 | 10 | At Mr Deane's school, Marylebone, London |
| c. 1700 | 12 | Family moves to Binfield, near Windsor, Berkshire |

# Chronology of his Times

| Year | Cultural Context | Historical Events |
|------|------------------|-------------------|
| 1688 | Death of John Bunyan | Glorious Revolution: James II deposed; accession of William of Orange (William III) |
| 1689 | John Locke, *Treatise on Civil Government* | James II in Ireland; Scottish Jacobites defeated at Killiecrankie |
| 1690 | Locke, *Essay Concerning Human Understanding* | James II defeated by William III at Battle of Boyne |
| 1694 | Purcell, *Te Deum* and *Jubilate* Congreve, *Double Dealer* | Death of Queen Mary; Bank of England founded |
| 1697 | Birth of Hogarth | Treaty of Ryswyck (England, France, Holland, Spain); Peter the Great of Russia visits England |
| 1698 | Vanbrugh, *The Provoked Wife* Fenelon, *Telemague* | George Lewis becomes Elector of Hanover (later English King George I) |
| 1700 | Death of John Dryden Congreve, *The Way of the World* | First American protest against slavery |
| 1701 | Steele, *The Christian Hero* | Act of Settlement; War of Spanish Succession begins; Yale College founded, New Haven, Conn. |
| 1702 | First English daily newspaper Daniel Defoe, *Shortest Way with Dissenters* (D in pillory) | Death of William III; accession of Anne |

| Year | Age | Life |
| --- | --- | --- |
| c. 1704 | 16 | In London learning French and Italian |
| c. 1705 | 17 | Begins acquaintance with London literary scene |
| 1709 | 20 | 2 May, *Pastorals* published in Tonson's *Poetical Miscellanies*; already knows Teresa and Martha Blount |
| 1711 | 22 | 15 May, *An Essay on Criticism* |
| 1712 | 23–4 | 14 May, *Messiah* published in *The Spectator*; 20 May, first version of *The Rape of the Lock*; Pope acquainted with Swift, Gay, Parnell, Arbuthnot (the Scriblerus Club) |
| 1713 | 24–5 | 7 March, *Windsor-Forest*; October, proposals for *Iliad* translation issued; Pope already intimate with Edward Harley, Earl of Oxford and Henry St John, Viscount Bolingbroke |
| 1714 | 25 | 4 March, 5-canto version of *The Rape of the Lock* published |
| 1715 | 26–7 | February, *The Temple of Fame*; 6 June, *Iliad*, vol. 1; gets to know Lady Mary Wortley Montagu |

| Year | Cultural Context | Historical Events |
| --- | --- | --- |
| 1704 | Swift, *Battle of the Books*, *Tale of a Tub* Newton, *Optics* | Duke of Marlborough defeats French at Bleinheim |
| 1705 | Mandeville, *Fable of the Bees* Vanbrugh begins Blenheim Palace | Parliament has Whig majority |
| 1707 | Farquar, *The Beaux Stratagem* Watts, *Hymns* London Society of Antiquaries | Union of England, Wales and Scotland as Great Britain |
| 1709 | Berkeley, *A New Theory of Vision* Steele, *The Tatler* (to 1711) | Marlborough defeats French at Malplaquet; Peter the Great defeats Charles XII of Sweden at Poltava |
| 1710 | Handel, *Rinaldo* (opera) Berkeley, *Principles of Human Knowledge* | English South Sea Company formed; Whig ministry falls; Tories form ministry under Harley and St John |
| 1711 | Shaftesbury, *Characteristics* Steele and Addison, *The Spectator* | Marlborough dismissed |
| 1712 | Arbuthnot, *History of John Bull* | St John becomes Viscount Bolingbroke; last English execution for witchcraft; Peace Congress begins at Utrecht |
| 1713 | Addison and Steele, *The Guardian* | |
| 1714 | | Fahrenheit's mercury thermometer; death of Queen Anne (August); accession of George I; Whigs in power; War of Spanish Succession ends |
| 1715 | Le Sage, *Gil Blas* Death of Fénelon | Bolingbroke to France; Jacobite rebellion (defeated at Preston and Sheriffmuir) |

| Year | Age | Life |
|------|-----|------|
| 1716 | 27 | 22 March, *Iliad*, vol. 2; enmity with publisher Edmund Curll; April, family move from Binfield to Chiswick, London |
| 1717 | 29 | 3 June, *Iliad*, vol. 3 and *Works* (containing *Eloisa to Abelard* and *Elegy to the Memory of an Unfortunate Lady*); 23 October, death of father |
| 1718 | 30 | 28 June, *Iliad*, vol. 4; moves with aged mother to neo-Palladian villa on Thames at Twickenham, Middlesex |
| 1720 | 31 | 12 May, *Iliad*, vols 5 and 6 |
| 1723 | 34 | January, edn of *Works* of John Sheffield, Duke of Buckingham, published but seized by government on suspicion of pro-Jacobite bias; early May, testifies before House of Lords on behalf of Bishop of Rochester (Atterbury), accused of Jacobitism |
| 1725 | 36 | 12 March, edn of Shakespeare (6 vols); 23 April, *The Odyssey* trans., vols 1–3 |
| 1726 | 37–8 | March, Lewis Theobald secures Pope's enmity with attack on Pope's Shakespeare; June, *The Odyssey* trans., vols 4–5; visit from Swift |
| 1727 | 39 | June, Pope–Swift *Miscellanies in Verse and Prose*, vols 1–2; another Swift visit |
| 1728 | 39 | 8 March, Pope–Swift *Miscellanies. The Last Volume*; 18 May, *The Dunciad. An Heroic Poem. In Three Books* |
| 1729 | 40 | 10 April, *The Dunciad Variorum* |

| Year | Cultural Context | Historical Events |
|------|------------------|-------------------|
| 1716 | Death of Leibniz<br>Birth of Thomas Gray | 'James III' (Old Pretender) in Scotland |
| 1717 | Union of English Freemasons<br>Grand Lodge founded | Robert Walpole resigns; Triple Alliance (England, France, Holland) |
| 1718 | | Lady Mary Wortley Montagu introduces inoculation against smallpox |
| 1720 | Handel, *Esther*<br>Death of Anne Finch, Countess of Winchilsea | South Sea Bubble bursts |
| 1721 | Nathan Bailey's *Etymological English Dictionary*<br>Gibbs starts St Martin's in the Fields | Walpole appointed first Lord of Treasury and Chancellor of Exchequer |
| 1723 | Birth of Reynolds<br>Death of Wren | Bolingbroke back from exile |
| 1725 | | Death of Peter the Great; Guy's Hospital founded |
| 1726 | Swift, *Gulliver's Travels*<br>First circulating library in Edinburgh<br>Defoe, *Voyages of Captain George Roberts* | |
| 1727 | Birth of Gainsborough<br>Death of Newton | Death of George I (June); accession of George II; siege of Gibraltar (England, Spain) |
| 1728 | Gay, *Beggar's Opera* | |
| 1729 | J. S. Bach, *St Matthew Passion* | Treaty of Seville (England, Spain, Holland); the Carolinas become Crown colonies |

| Year | Age | Life |
|------|-----|------|
| 1731 | 43 | December, *Of Taste: An Epistle to the Right Honourable Richard, Earl of Burlington* (becomes Moral Essay 4) |
| 1732 | 44 | 4 October, Pope–Swift *Miscellanies. The Third Volume* |
| 1733 | 44–5 | 15 January, *Of the Use of Riches: An Epistle to the Right Honourable Allen, Lord Bathurst* (Moral Essay 3); 15 February, *The First Satire of the Second Book of Horace, Imitated*; February–May, *An Essay on Man*, Epistles 1–3; 7 June, death of mother |
| 1734 | 45–6 | 16 January, *An Epistle to the Right Honourable Richard, Lord Viscount Cobham* (Moral Essay 1); 24 January, *An Essay on Man*, Epistle 4; 4 July, *Imitations of Horace*, Satires 2.2; 28 December, *Sober Advice from Horace* |
| 1735 | 46 | 2 February, *An Epistle from Mr Pope to Dr Arbuthnot*; 8 February, *Of the Characters of Women: An Epistle to a Lady* (Moral Essay 2); 23 April, *Works*, vol. 2; 12 May, Curll's edn of Pope's *Letters* |
| 1737 | 48–9 | 28 April, *Imitations of Horace*, Epistle 2.2; 19 May, own edition of *Letters*; 25 May, *Imitations of Horace*, Epistle 2.1 |
| 1738 | 49–50 | 23 January, *Imitations of Horace*, Epistle 1.6; 1 March, *Imitations of Horace*, Satire 2.6; 7 March, *Imitations of Horace*, Epistle 1.1; 16 May, *One Thousand Seven Hundred and Thirty-Eight. A Dialogue Something like Horace*; 22 June, *The Universal Prayer*; 18 July, *One Thousand Seven Hundred and Thirty-Eight. Dialogue 2* |

| Year | Cultural Context | Historical Events |
|---|---|---|
| 1730 | Thomson, *The Seasons* and *Sophonisba*; *The Grub Street Journal* (till 1737) | Walpole and Charles, Viscount Townshend quarrel; Townshend resigns |
| 1731 | *Gentleman's Magazine* begins<br>Death of Defoe<br>Hogarth, *A Harlot's Progress* | |
| 1732 | Berkeley, *Dialogues of Alciphron*<br>Voltaire, *Zaire* | Colony of Georgia founded; Boerhaave founds organic chemistry |
| 1733 | Prévost, *Manon Lescaut*<br>Bach, *B minor Mass* | American colonies forbidden to trade with French West Indies |
| 1734 | Voltaire, *Lettres sur les Anglais*<br>Bach, *Christmas Oratorio* | Commercial treaty between England and Russia |
| 1735 | (February) Death of Arbuthnot<br>Thomson, *Liberty*<br>Linnaeus, *Systema naturae*<br>Hogarth, *A Rake's Progress* | Copyright Act in England |
| 1737 | | Licensing Act (all plays open to censorship by Lord Chamberlain) |
| 1738 | Handel, *Saul* | John Wesley and George Whitefield start Methodism; Paul's spinning machine patented in England; Pope Clement XII bans freemasonry |

| Year | Age | Life |
|------|-----|------|
| 1739 | 51 | November (to February 1740) begins series of winter stays with Ralph Allen at Prior Park, Bath |
| 1740 | 51 | April, beginning of Pope's friendship with William Warburton, Bishop of Gloucester |
| 1742 | 53 | 20 March, *The New Dunciad* |
| 1743 | 55 | 29 October, *The Dunciad, in Four Books* |
| 1744 | 56 | 30 May, death of Pope |

| Year | Cultural Context | Historical Events |
|---|---|---|
| 1739 | Hume, *Treatise on Human Nature* | England declares war on Spain |
| 1740 | Thomson (with David Mallett), *Alfred* (contains 'Rule, Britannia') <br> Samuel Richardson, *Pamela* | |
| 1742 | Henry Fielding, *Joseph Andrews* <br> Edward Young, *Night Thoughts* <br> Gray begins *Elegy* <br> Handel, *Messiah*, performed | Walpole resigns, succeeded by Sir Spenser Compton, Earl of Wilmington; John Carteret, Lord Granville, Secretary of State |
| 1743 | Handel, *Samson* | Death of Wilmington; Henry Pelham succeeds as First Lord of the Treasury; England defeats French at Dettingen; Treaty of Worms (England, Austria, |
| 1744 | Hogarth, *Marriage à la Mode* <br> Birth of William Hodges (landscape painter) | Fall of Carteret; France declares war on England; Clive arrives at Madras |

# Introduction

Alexander Pope was an inheritor of the blending of Christianity with ancient learning that began with the Renaissance some two hundred years before his birth in 1688. For him, as for many of his friends and contemporaries, the rediscovery of the languages and achievements of the ancient world of Greece and Rome that had made such an impact on sixteenth-century European thought remained a legacy of inestimable value, revealing the ancients as repositories of living moral and artistic truth as they focused on man as a restlessly striving intellectual being attempting to place himself in relation to the gods and the cosmos. Although their humanising, optimistic and anthropocentric energies could not supplant Christianity's emphasis on collective and individual sin, they offered a salutary modification and softening of it, enabling humanity once again to justify its worldly ambitions and to take less seriously its failings and pomposities.

If this makes Pope sound reactionary, then this is because, from some points of view, he was. Temperamentally conservative, he valued authority, in church, state and the arts. Along with his friends Swift, Gay, Arbuthnot, Fielding and many more, he was terrified that a world without authority was chaos; that art without training and order – without an underlying philosophy or ethic – was no art and was therefore immoral. He believed, with his Renaissance forebears, that God created the world out of a system of elegant harmonies, and that the arts imitated the cosmic harmony just as the structures and proportions of the individual body and soul did. He would have mocked and fiercely despised the winners of the contemporary Turner prize, and post-modernism in its various literary and architectural manifestations. For him they would have been symptoms of cultural forgetting, of the amnesia that lets great achievement from the past cease to mean.

Pope was born into the Catholic religion of his parents and remained a Catholic all his life despite the penalties that this imposed on him: prohibitions on education, inheritance, the holding of public office, etc. Quietly rather than stridently Catholic, he numbered among his friends some of the leading (Protestant) figures of his day. His Catholicism nevertheless marginalised him: alongside his illness (tubercular bone infection led to gradual deformity and collapse of his spine and chest), it set him apart, making him more than psychologically ready to adopt (and revel in) the persona of the beleaguered satirist, the lone voice of truth in a nonsensical world.

Pope's moral, artistic and social ideal, mythologised from an idealised image of Rome under Augustus Caesar (whose reign spanned the birth of Christ), underpins nearly all his poetry. Augustus represented political peace and encouraged the arts, particularly the great epic poet, Virgil, and the architect Vitruvius (see note to *Epistle to Burlington*, line 194). In harking back to Augustan Rome, Pope was, of course, also recalling the equivalent revival during the Renaissance when, alongside the strengths of ancient philosophers, poets and sculptors, Vitruvian architectural theory had been rediscovered the first time round. Hence Pope makes Vitruvius and his sixteenth-century disciple Andrea Palladio (and Palladio's British disciple, Inigo Jones) central to the *Epistle to Burlington*, the poem which encodes Pope's obsession with taste as an index of cultural and moral value, using architecture and garden design – the right use of the land – as its main symbols. Indeed, land is perhaps more important than architecture in the poem, because for Pope as for Virgil it is the recipient of, and redemptive cure for, human folly. The site of battle and bloodshed with the Roman and the English Civil Wars, under a peace-bringing ruler its battle scars become furrows, soaked-in blood yields corn, and agricultural prosperity leads to the ultimate expression of civilisation, the building of cities (as in Virgil's *Georgics* and Pope's *Windsor-Forest*).

Unlike Virgil's Augustus, however, the monarch of *Windsor-Forest* is known to be an ailing woman, and one who was to die childless. So that, at the very moment he celebrates peace under his ideal ruler, the Protestant Stuart, Anne, Pope knows that the future is dark – for him as a Catholic (Anne had tolerated Catholicism in a way that her predecessor, William III, had not); for the country, because her successor (by the Act of Settlement, 1701) was to be the 54-year-old George, Elector of Hanover – a man, it was xenophobically rumoured, of no taste, with no interest in the language of his new country. Pope subscribed, at least emotionally, to the old idea of monarchs as supreme patrons, of the court as the arbiter of taste. If the monarch has no interest in the language of the country over which he rules, Pope gloomily predicted, then literature at least is doomed. (It also has to be said that his gloom at the prospect of Anne's death may well have been deepened by more than a tinge of Catholic Jacobitism (the term derives from Jacobus, Latin for James). Anne had been the daughter of the deposed Catholic James II; with the Protestant succession secured on George of Hanover, many felt that the crown belonged by right to James's surviving son, the exiled Catholic James Francis Edward (1688–1766), the Old Pretender.)

Pope's view of things darkened further with the accession of George II in 1727, by which time his literary and personal enemies had formed into a neatly coherent satirical target. The result was the first version of *The Dunciad* – a harshly brilliant pillorying of his enemies, and a horrified exposé of the corruption of the ideal of the city into London's mud and sewage. How he got away with its sixth line – 'Still Dunce the second reigns like Dunce the first' – we shall never know; but it devastatingly pinpoints the first two Georges of Hanover, and so, more generally, does the work's mock-epic structure. For mock-epic (that is, epic framework without the heroism, all turned to a joke) implies that whereas epic was once possible, it no longer is. Monarchs set the tone for the nation and its destiny – under Hanover epic is no longer possible, heroism is a thing of the past.

Much else had been contributing to the collapse of the heroic ideal; but the fact remains that Pope could write epic only by translating his predecessors. Where Milton could commemorate the Puritan republic, even after its defeat and his personal humiliation, in the magnificent blank verse epic *Paradise Lost* (1667), Pope could see no recent past – or present – to celebrate. So he translated the two works which mark the beginning of western European epic, Homer's *Iliad* and *Odyssey*, eventually proceeding to *The Dunciad*, which he was to tinker with, on and off, for the rest of his life. It is an expression of Tory pessimism at its most extreme; the last full lament for the death of Christianity and the ancient world as they had historically combined to produce Christian humanism. Heroism in this world exists only as opposition to the prevailing anti-culture; only, in fact, in the figure of the embattled, solitary, poet and the fragments of past literature which he incorporates into his work.

All this had been anticipated as early as *The Rape of the Lock*. For if *The Dunciad* is the exact opposite of *Windsor-Forest* (dirty Hanoverian cityscape instead of ideal Stuart country, etc.), the mock heroics of *The Rape of the Lock* in its expanded (1714) form, too, are the opposite of *Windsor-Forest*. We are now a little further down the Thames – no longer at Windsor but at Hampton Court – and Anne is still alive, but only just (she was to die 1 August 1714). So, with memories of Homer, Virgil and others, Belinda the Sun Queen parodies monarchical power and ends up eclipsed, the melancholic loser of her lock of hair and of her authority. Pope continues the elegiac note (without the comedy) in his next major poems (apart from the *Iliad* translation), *Eloisa to Abelard* – the story of a woman mourning her lost life and love – and the *Elegy to the Memory of an Unfortunate Lady*. It is as if Anne's death caused Pope to be haunted by grieving women. Later, in *The Dunciad*, grief will turn to comic grotesquerie and terrible absurdity as the Georges are seen to have produced a travestied Anne in the dark goddess, Dullness.

Pope's nostalgia is a strong thing and his poetic voice is always assertive. Shot through with images of loss, disease and corruption as his poetry is, the verse – modelled on Dryden's, though more technically assured – is always elegant, balanced, precise. Pope's heroic couplets (two lines of ten syllables, almost invariably with an iambic rhythm, each of the pairs of lines rhyming with itself) surmount personal sickness and imagined terrors to affirm his fundamental view of civilisation as order.

DOUGLAS BROOKS-DAVIES

# Alexander Pope

# Windsor-Forest

## To the Right Honourable George Lord Lansdowne

Thy forests, Windsor, and thy green retreats,
At once the monarch's and the Muse's seats,
Invite my lays. Be present, sylvan maids!
Unlock your springs, and open all your shades.
Granville commands; your aid, O Muses, bring!       5
What Muse for Granville can refuse to sing?
   The groves of Eden, vanished now so long,
Live in description, and look green in song:
These, were my breast inspired with equal flame,
Like them in beauty, should be like in fame.       10
Here hills and vales, the woodland and the plain,
Here earth and water seem to strive again –
Not chaos-like together crushed and bruised,
But, as the world, harmoniously confused:
Where order in variety we see,       15
And where, though all things differ, all agree.
Here waving groves a chequered scene display,
And part admit, and part exclude, the day,
As some coy nymph her lover's warm address
Nor quite indulges, nor can quite repress.       20
There, interspersed in lawns and opening glades,
Thin trees arise that shun each other's shades.
Here in full light the russet plains extend;
There, wrapped in clouds, the blueish hills ascend.
Even the wild heath displays her purple dyes,       25
And 'midst the desert fruitful fields arise
That, crowned with tufted trees and springing corn,
Like verdant isles the sable waste adorn.
Let India boast her plants, nor envy we
The weeping amber or the balmy tree       30
While, by our oaks, the precious loads are borne,
And realms commanded which those trees adorn.
Not proud Olympus yields a nobler sight,

Though gods assembled grace his towering height,
Than what more humble mountains offer here,                    35
Where, in their blessings, all those gods appear.
See Pan with flocks, with fruits Pomona crowned;
Here blushing Flora paints th'enamelled ground;
Here Ceres' gifts in waving prospect stand,
And nodding tempt the joyful reaper's hand;                    40
Rich Industry sits smiling on the plains,
And peace and plenty tell, a STUART reigns.
    Not thus the land appeared in ages past:
A dreary desert and a gloomy waste,
To savage beasts and savage laws a prey,                       45
And kings more furious and severe than they,
Who claimed the skies, dispeopled air and floods,
The lonely lords of empty wilds and woods.
Cities laid waste, they stormed the dens and caves
(For wiser brutes were backward to be slaves).                 50
What could be free when lawless beasts obeyed,
And even the elements a tyrant swayed?
In vain kind seasons swelled the teeming grain;
Soft showers distilled, and suns grew warm, in vain:
The swain with tears his frustrate labour yields,             55
And famished dies amidst his ripened fields.
What wonder, then, a beast or subject slain
Were equal crimes in a despotic reign,
Both doomed alike, for sportive tyrants bled;
But while the subject starved, the beast was fed.            60
Proud Nimrod first the bloody chase began –
A mighty hunter, and his prey was man:
Our haughty Norman boasts that barbarous name,
And makes his trembling slaves the royal game.
The fields are ravished from th'industrious swains,         65
From men their cities, and from gods their fanes:
The levelled towns with weeds lie covered o'er;
The hollow winds through naked temples roar;
Round broken columns clasping ivy twined;
O'er heaps of ruin stalked the stately hind;                70
The fox obscene to gaping tombs retires,
And savage howlings fill the sacred choirs.
Awed by his nobles, by his commons cursed,

The oppressor ruled tyrannic where he durst,
Stretched o'er the poor and Church his iron rod,                     75
And served alike his vassals and his god:
Whom even the Saxon spared and bloody Dane,
The wanton victims of his sport remain.
But see the man who spacious regions gave
A waste for beasts, himself denied a grave!                          80
Stretched on the lawn his second hope survey,
At once the chaser, and at once the prey:
Lo, Rufus, tugging at the deadly dart,
Bleeds in the forest like a wounded hart.
Succeeding monarchs heard the subjects' cries,                       85
Nor saw displeased the peaceful cottage rise.
Then gathering flocks on unknown mountains fed,
O'er sandy wilds were yellow harvests spread,
The forests wondered at the unusual grain,
And secret transport touched the conscious swain:                    90
Fair Liberty, Britannia's Goddess, rears
Her cheerful head, and leads the golden years.

Ye vigorous swains: while youth ferments your blood,
And purer spirits swell the spritely flood,
Now range the hills, the gameful woods beset,                        95
Wind the shrill horn, or spread the waving net.
When milder autumn summer's heat succeeds,
And in the new-shorn field the partridge feeds,
Before his lord the ready spaniel bounds:
Panting with hope he tries the furrowed grounds,                     100
But when the tainted gales the game betray,
Couched close he lies, and meditates the prey:
Secure they trust the unfaithful field, beset,
'Till hovering o'er 'em sweeps the swelling net.
Thus (if small things we may with great compare),                    105
When Albion sends her eager sons to war,
Some thoughtless town, with ease and plenty blessed,
Near, and more near, the closing lines invest;
Sudden they seize the amazed, defenceless prize,
And high in air Britannia's standard flies.                          110

See, from the brake the whirring pheasant springs,
And mounts exulting on triumphant wings:
Short is his joy; he feels the fiery wound,

Flutters in blood, and panting beats the ground.
Ah, what avail his glossy, varying dyes,                              115
His purple crest and scarlet-circled eyes,
The vivid green his shining plumes unfold,
His painted wings, and breast that flames with gold?
    Nor yet, when moist Arcturus clouds the sky,
The woods and fields their pleasing toils deny;                      120
To plains with well-breathed beagles we repair,
And trace the mazes of the circling hare
(Beasts, urged by us, their fellow beasts pursue,
And learn of man each other to undo).
With slaughtering guns the unwearied fowler roves                    125
(When frosts have whitened all the naked groves)
Where doves in flocks the leafless trees o'ershade,
And lonely woodcocks haunt the watery glade.
He lifts the tube and levels with his eye –
Straight a short thunder breaks the frozen sky.                      130
Oft, as in airy rings they skim the heath,
The clamorous lapwings feel the leaden death;
Oft, as the mounting larks their notes prepare,
They fall, and leave their little lives in air.
    In genial spring, beneath the quivering shade,                   135
Where cooling vapours breathe along the mead,
The patient fisher takes his silent stand,
Intent, his angle trembling in his hand:
With looks unmoved he hopes the scaly breed,
And eyes the dancing cork and bending reed.                          140
Our plenteous streams a various race supply –
The bright-eyed perch with fins of Tyrian dye;
The silver eel, in shining volumes rolled;
The yellow carp, in scales bedropped with gold;
Swift trouts, diversified with crimson stains;                       145
And pikes, the tyrants of the watery plains.
    Now Cancer glows with Phœbus' fiery car:
The youth rush eager to the sylvan war,
Swarm o'er the lawns, the forest walks surround,
Rouse the fleet hart, and cheer the opening hound.                   150
The impatient courser pants in every vein,
And pawing, seems to beat the distant plain:
Hills, vales, and floods appear already crossed

And, e'er he starts, a thousand steps are lost.
See the bold youth strain up the threatening steep, 155
Rush through the thickets, down the valleys sweep,
Hang o'er their coursers' heads with eager speed,
And earth rolls back beneath the flying steed.
Let old Arcadia boast her ample plain,
The immortal huntress, and her virgin train; 160
Nor envy, Windsor, since thy shades have seen
As bright a goddess and as chaste a queen,
Whose care, like hers, protects the sylvan reign,
The earth's fair light, and empress of the main.
     Here too, 'tis sung, of old Diana strayed, 165
And Cynthus' top forsook for Windsor shade:
Here was she seen o'er airy wastes to rove,
Seek the clear spring, or haunt the pathless grove;
Here, armed with silver bows, in early dawn,
Her buskined virgins traced the dewy lawn. 170
     Above the rest a rural nymph was famed –
Thy offspring, Thames, the fair Lodona named
(Lodona's fate, in long oblivion cast,
The Muse shall sing, and what she sings shall last).
Scarce could the goddess from her nymph be known 175
But by the crescent and the golden zone:
She scorned the praise of beauty, and the care;
A belt her waist, a fillet binds her hair;
A painted quiver on her shoulder sounds,
And with her dart the flying deer she wounds. 180
It chanced as, eager of the chase, the maid
Beyond the forest's verdant limits strayed,
Pan saw and loved and, burning with desire,
Pursued her flight – her flight increased his fire.
Not half so swift the trembling doves can fly 185
When the fierce eagle cleaves the liquid sky;
Not half so swiftly the fierce eagle moves
When, through the clouds, he drives the trembling doves,
As from the god she flew with furious pace,
Or as the god, more furious, urged the chase. 190
Now fainting, sinking, pale, the nymph appears;
Now close behind his sounding steps she hears;
And now his shadow reached her as she run

(His shadow, lengthened by the setting sun);
And now his shorter breath, with sultry air,                    195
Pants on her neck, and fans her parting hair.
In vain on father Thames she calls for aid,
Nor could Diana help her injured maid.
Faint, breathless, thus she prayed, nor prayed in vain:
'Ah, Cynthia, ah – though banished from thy train,             200
Let me, oh let me to the shades repair –
My native shades – there weep and murmur there.'
She said, and melting as in tears she lay,
In a soft, silver stream dissolved away.
The silver stream her virgin coldness keeps,                   205
For ever murmurs, and for ever weeps;
Still bears the name the hapless virgin bore,
And bathes the forest where she ranged before:
In her chaste current oft the goddess laves,
And with celestial tears augments the waves;                   210
Oft in her glass the musing shepherd spies
The headlong mountains and the downward skies,
The watery landscape of the pendant woods,
And absent trees that tremble in the floods:
In the clear azure gleam the flocks are seen,                  215
And floating forests paint the waves with green.
Through the fair scene roll slow the lingering streams,
Then foaming pour along, and rush into the Thames.
     Thou, too, great father of the British floods,
With joyful pride surveyest our lofty woods,                   220
Where towering oaks their growing honours rear,
And future navies on thy shores appear.
Not Neptune's self from all her streams receives
A wealthier tribute than to thine he gives.
No seas so rich, so gay no banks appear,                       225
No lake so gentle, and no spring so clear.
Nor Po so swells the fabling poet's lays,
While led along the skies his current strays,
As thine, which visits Windsor's famed abodes
To grace the mansion of our earthly gods.                      230
Nor all his stars above a lustre show
Like the bright beauties on thy banks below,
Where Jove, subdued by mortal passion still,

Might change Olympus for a nobler hill.
  Happy the man whom this bright court approves,     235
His sovereign favours, and his country loves:
Happy next him who to these shades retires,
Whom Nature charms, and whom the Muse inspires,
Whom humbler joys of home-felt quiet please –
Successive study, exercise, and ease.     240
He gathers health from herbs the forest yields,
And of their fragrant physic spoils the fields;
With chemic art exalts the mineral powers,
And draws the aromatic souls of flowers;
Now marks the course of rolling orbs on high;     245
O'er figured worlds now travels with his eye;
Of ancient writ unlocks the learned store;
Consults the dead, and lives past ages o'er.
Or, wandering thoughtful in the silent wood,
Attends the duties of the wise and good,     250
To observe a mean, be to himself a friend,
To follow nature, and regard his end;
Or looks on heaven with more than mortal eyes,
Bids his free soul expatiate in the skies,
Amid her kindred stars familiar roam,     255
Survey the region, and confess her home!
Such was the life great Scipio once admired –
Thus Atticus, and Trumbull thus retired.
  Ye sacred nine, that all my soul possess,
Whose raptures fire me, and whole visions bless,     260
Bear me, oh bear me to sequestered scenes,
The bowery mazes, and surrounding greens:
To Thames's banks, which fragrant breezes fill,
Or where ye Muses sport on Cooper's Hill
(On Cooper's Hill eternal wreaths shall grow,     265
While lasts the mountain, or while Thames shall flow).
I seem through consecrated walks to rove,
I hear soft music die along the grove;
Led by the sound I roam from shade to shade,
By godlike poets venerable made:     270
Here his first lays majestic Denham sung;
There the last numbers flowed from Cowley's tongue.
Oh early lost! What tears the river shed

When the sad pomp along his banks was led!
His drooping swans on every note expire, 275
And on his willows hung each Muse's lyre.
  Since fate relentless stopped their heavenly voice,
No more the forests ring, or groves rejoice:
Who now shall charm the shades, where Cowley strung
His living harp, and lofty Denham sung? 280
But hark! The groves rejoice, the forest rings –
Are these revived, or is it Granville sings?
'Tis yours, my lord, to bless our soft retreats,
And call the Muses to their ancient seats,
To paint anew the flowery sylvan scenes, 285
To crown the forests with immortal greens,
Make Windsor hills in lofty numbers rise,
And lift her turrets nearer to the skies:
To sing those honours you deserve to wear,
And add new lustre to her silver star. 290
  Here noble Surrey felt the sacred rage –
Surrey, the Granville of a former age:
Matchless his pen, victorious was his lance,
Bold in the lists, and graceful in the dance;
In the same shades the Cupids tuned his lyre 295
To the same notes of love and soft desire:
Fair Geraldine, bright object of his vow,
Then filled the groves, as heavenly Myra now.
  Oh, wouldest thou sing what heroes Windsor bore,
What kings first breathed upon her winding shore, 300
Or raise old warriors, whose adored remains
In weeping vaults her hallowed earth contains!
With Edward's acts adorn the shining page,
Stretch his long triumphs down through every age,
Draw monarchs chained, and Cressy's glorious field, 305
The lilies blazing on the regal shield:
Then, from her roofs, when Verrio's colours fall,
And leave inanimate the naked wall,
Still in thy song should vanquished France appear,
And bleed for ever under Britain's spear. 310
  Let softer strains ill-fated Henry mourn,
And palms eternal flourish round his urn:
Here o'er the martyr-king the marble weeps,

And fast beside him once-feared Edward sleeps:
Whom not th'extended Albion could contain,                    315
From old Bellerium to the northern main,
The grave unites, where even the great find rest,
And blended lie the oppressor and the oppressed.
   Make sacred Charles's tomb for ever known
(Obscure the place, and uninscribed the stone):              320
Oh fact accursed! What tears has Albion shed,
Heavens, what new wounds! And how her old have bled!
She saw her sons with purple deaths expire,
Her sacred domes involved in rolling fire,
A dreadful series of intestine wars,                          325
Inglorious triumphs and dishonest scars.
At length great Anna said 'Let Discord cease!'
She said, the world obeyed, and all was peace.
   In that blessed moment from his oozy bed
Old father Thames advanced his reverend head.                330
His tresses dropped with dews, and o'er the stream
His shining horns diffused a golden gleam.
Graved on his urn appeared the moon, that guides
His swelling waters and alternate tides;
The figured streams in waves of silver rolled,               335
And on their banks Augusta rose in gold.
Around his throne the sea-born brothers stood
Who swell with tributary urns his flood:
First, the famed authors of his ancient name,
The winding Isis and the fruitful Thame;                      340
The Kennet swift, for silver eels renowned;
The Loddon slow, with verdant alders crowned;
Cole, whose dark streams his flowery islands lave;
And chalky Wey, that rolls a milky wave;
The blue, transparent Vandalis appears;                       345
The gulfy Lee his sedgy tresses rears;
And sullen Mole, that hides his diving flood;
And silent Darent, stained with Danish blood.
   High in the midst, upon his urn reclined
(His sea-green mantle waving with the wind),                  350
The god appeared. He turned his azure eyes
Where Windsor domes and pompous turrets rise,
Then bowed and spoke: the winds forget to roar,

And the hushed waves glide softly to the shore.
   'Hail, sacred Peace! Hail long-expected days,     355
That Thames's glory to the stars shall raise!
Though Tiber's streams immortal Rome behold,
Though foaming Hermus swells with tides of gold,
From heaven itself though sevenfold Nilus flows
And harvests on a hundred realms bestows,     360
These now no more shall be the Muse's themes,
Lost in my fame, as in the sea their streams.
Let Volga's banks with iron squadrons shine,
And groves of lances glitter on the Rhine;
Let barbarous Ganges arm a servile train –     365
Be mine the blessings of a peaceful reign.
No more my sons shall dye with British blood
Red Iber's sands, or Ister's foaming flood:
Safe on my shore each unmolested swain
Shall tend the flocks, or reap the bearded grain.     370
The shady empire shall retain no trace
Of war or blood but in the sylvan chase;
The trumpets sleep while cheerful horns are blown,
And arms employed on birds and beasts alone.
Behold, the ascending villas on my side     375
Project long shadows o'er the crystal tide.
Behold, Augusta's glittering spires increase,
And temples rise, the beauteous works of peace.
I see, I see where two fair cities bend
Their ample bow, a new Whitehall ascend!     380
There mighty nations shall enquire their doom,
The world's great oracle in times to come;
There kings shall sue, and suppliant states be seen
Once more to bend before a British Queen.
   Thy trees, fair Windsor, now shall leave their woods,     385
And half thy forests rush into my floods,
Bear Britain's thunder, and her cross display
To the bright regions of the rising day;
Tempt icy seas, where scarce the waters roll,
Where clearer flames glow round the frozen Pole;     390
Or under southern skies exalt their sails,
Led by new stars, and borne by spicy gales!
For me the balm shall bleed, and amber flow,

The coral redden, and the ruby glow,
The pearly shell its lucid globe enfold,                              395
And Phœbus warm the ripening ore to gold.
The time shall come when, free as seas or wind,
Unbounded Thames shall flow for all mankind,
Whole nations enter with each swelling tide,
And seas but join the regions they divide;                           400
Earth's distant ends our glory shall behold,
And the new world launch forth to seek the old.
Then ships of uncouth form shall stem the tide,
And feathered people crowd my wealthy side,
And naked youths and painted chiefs admire                           405
Our speech, our colour, and our strange attire!
Oh stretch thy reign, fair Peace, from shore to shore,
'Till conquest cease, and slavery be no more,
'Till the freed Indians in their native groves
Reap their own fruits and woo their sable loves,                     410
Peru once more a race of kings behold,
And other Mexicos be roofed with gold.
Exiled by thee from earth to deepest hell,
In brazen bonds shall barbarous Discord dwell;
Gigantic Pride, pale Terror, gloomy Care,                            415
And mad Ambition shall attend her there.
There purple Vengeance, bathed in gore, retires,
Her weapons blunted, and extinct her fires;
There hateful Envy her own snakes shall feel,
And Persecution mourn her broken wheel;                              420
There Faction roar, Rebellion bite her chain,
And gasping Furies thirst for blood in vain.'
   Here cease thy flight, nor with unhallowed lays
Touch the fair fame of Albion's golden days:
The thoughts of gods let Granville's verse recite,                   425
And bring the scenes of opening fate to light.
My humble Muse, in unambitious strains,
Paints the green forests and the flowery plains,
Where Peace, descending, bids her olives spring,
And scatters blessings from her dove-like wing.                      430
Even I more sweetly pass my careless days,
Pleased in the silent shade with empty praise;
Enough for me that, to the listening swains,
First in these fields I sung the sylvan strains.

# The Rape of the Lock

## CANTO 1

What dire offence from amorous causes springs,
What mighty contests rise from trivial things,
I sing. This verse to Caryll, Muse, is due;
This even Belinda may vouchsafe to view:
Slight is the subject, but not so the praise,          5
If she inspire, and he approve, my lays.
　Say what strange motive, goddess, could compel
A well-bred lord to assault a gentle belle?
Oh, say what stranger cause, yet unexplored,
Could make a gentle belle reject a lord?          10
In tasks so bold can little men engage,
And in soft bosoms dwells such mighty rage?
　Sol through white curtains shot a timorous ray,
And oped those eyes that must eclipse the day;
Now lap-dogs give themselves the rousing shake,          15
And sleepless lovers, just at twelve, awake;
Thrice rung the bell, the slipper knocked the ground,
And the pressed watch returned a silver sound.
Belinda still her downy pillow pressed,
Her guardian sylph prolonged the balmy rest:          20
'Twas he had summoned to her silent bed
The morning dream that hovered o'er her head.
A youth more glittering than a birth-night beau
(That even in slumber caused her cheek to glow)
Seemed to her ear his winning lips to lay,          25
And thus in whispers said, or seemed to say:
　'Fairest of mortals, thou distinguished care
Of thousand bright inhabitants of air!
If e'er one vision touched thy infant thought
Of all the nurse and all the priest have taught          30
Of airy elves by moonlight shadows seen,
The silver token, and the circled green,
Or virgins visited by angel-powers,
With golden crowns and wreaths of heavenly flowers,

Hear and believe: thy own importance know,                    35
Nor bound thy narrow views to things below.
Some secret truths, from learned pride concealed,
To maids alone and children are revealed.
What though no credit doubting wits may give –
The fair and innocent shall still believe.                    40
Know then, unnumbered spirits round thee fly,
The light militia of the lower sky;
These, though unseen, are ever on the wing,
Hang o'er the box, and hover round the Ring:
Think what an equipage thou hast in air,                      45
And view with scorn two pages and a chair.
As now your own, our beings were of old,
And once enclosed in woman's beauteous mould;
Thence, by a soft transition, we repair
From earthly vehicles to these of air.                        50
Think not, when woman's transient breath is fled,
That all her vanities at once are dead:
Succeeding vanities she still regards
And, though she plays no more, o'erlooks the cards.
Her joy in gilded chariots when alive,                        55
And love of ombre, after death survive.
For when the fair in all their pride expire,
To their first elements their souls retire:
The sprites of fiery termagants in flame
Mount up, and take a salamander's name;                       60
Soft yielding minds to water glide away,
And sip with nymphs their elemental tea;
The graver prude sinks downward to a gnome,
In search of mischief still on earth to roam;
The light coquettes in sylphs aloft repair,                   65
And sport and flutter in the fields of air.
    Know farther yet: whoever, fair and chaste,
Rejects mankind is by some sylph embraced;
For spirits, freed from mortal laws, with ease
Assume what sexes and what shapes they please.                70
What guards the purity of melting maids
In courtly balls and midnight masquerades,
Safe from the treacherous friend, the daring spark,
The glance by day, the whisper in the dark,

When kind occasion prompts their warm desires,                75
When music softens, and when dancing fires?
'Tis but their sylph, the wise celestials know,
Though "honour" is the word with men below.
    Some nymphs there are, too conscious of their face,
For life predestined to the gnomes' embrace:                  80
These swell their prospects and exalt their pride
When offers are disdained, and love denied.
Then gay ideas crowd the vacant brain,
While peers and dukes, and all their sweeping train,
And garters, stars, and coronets appear,                      85
And in soft sounds, "Your Grace" salutes their ear.
'Tis these that early taint the female soul,
Instruct the eyes of young coquettes to roll,
Teach infant cheeks a bidden blush to know,
And little hearts to flutter at a beau.                        90
    Oft, when the world imagine women stray,
The sylphs through mystic mazes guide their way
Through all the giddy circle they pursue,
And old impertinence expel by new.
What tender maid but must a victim fall                        95
To one man's treat, but for another's ball?
When Florio speaks, what virgin could withstand,
If gentle Damon did not squeeze her hand?
With varying vanities, from every part,
They shift the moving toyshop of their heart,                 100
Where wigs with wigs, with sword-knots sword-knots strive,
Beaus banish beaus, and coaches coaches drive.
This erring mortals "levity" may call:
Oh, blind to truth! The sylphs contrive it all.
    Of these am I, who thy protection claim,                  105
A watchful sprite, and Ariel is my name.
Late, as I ranged the crystal wilds of air,
In the clear mirror of thy ruling star
I saw, alas, some dread event impend,
Ere to the main this morning sun descend,                     110
But heaven reveals not what, or how, or where.
Warned by the sylph, oh pious maid, beware!
This to disclose is all thy guardian can:
Beware of all, but most beware of man!'

He said; when Shock, who thought she slept too long,          115
Leaped up, and waked his mistress with his tongue.
'Twas then Belinda, if report say true,
Thy eyes first opened on a billet-doux:
Wounds, charms, and ardours were no sooner read,
But all the vision vanished from thy head.                    120
    And now, unveiled, the toilette stands displayed,
Each silver vase in mystic order laid.
First, robed in white, the nymph intent adores,
With head uncovered, the cosmetic powers.
A heavenly image in the glass appears –                       125
To that she bends, to that her eyes she rears;
The inferior priestess, at her altar's side,
Trembling, begins the sacred rites of pride.
Unnumbered treasures ope at once, and here
The various offerings of the world appear;                    130
From each she nicely culls with curious toil,
And decks the goddess with the glittering spoil.
This casket India's glowing gems unlocks,
And all Arabia breathes from yonder box.
The tortoise here and elephant unite,                         135
Transformed to combs, the speckled, and the white.
Here files of pins extend their shining rows,
Puffs, powders, patches, Bibles, billets-doux.
Now awful Beauty puts on all its arms;
The fair each moment rises in her charms,                     140
Repairs her smiles, awakens every grace,
And calls forth all the wonders of her face;
Sees by degrees a purer blush arise,
And keener lightnings quicken in her eyes.
The busy sylphs surround their darling care –                 145
These set the head, and those divide the hair;
Some fold the sleeve, whilst others plait the gown,
And Betty's praised for labours not her own.


CANTO 2

Not with more glories, in th'etherial plain,
The sun first rises o'er the purpled main
Than, issuing forth, the rival of his beams

Launched on the bosom of the silver Thames.
Fair nymphs, and well-dressed youths around her shone,          5
But every eye was fixed on her alone.
On her white breast a sparkling cross she wore,
Which Jews might kiss, and infidels adore.
Her lively looks a spritely mind disclose,
Quick as her eyes, and as unfixed as those:          10
Favours to none, to all she smiles extends;
Oft she rejects, but never once offends.
Bright as the sun her eyes the gazers strike
And, like the sun, they shine on all alike.
Yet graceful ease, and sweetness void of pride,          15
Might hide her faults, if belles had faults to hide:
If to her share some female errors fall,
Look on her face, and you'll forget 'em all.
    This nymph, to the destruction of mankind,
Nourished two locks, which graceful hung behind          20
In equal curls, and well conspired to deck
With shining ringlets her smooth ivory neck.
Love in these labyrinths his slaves detains,
And mighty hearts are held in slender chains.
With hairy springes we the birds betray,          25
Slight lines of hair surprise the finny prey,
Fair tresses man's imperial race ensnare,
And beauty draws us with a single hair.
    The adventurous baron the bright locks admired:
He saw, he wished, and to the prize aspired.          30
Resolved to win, he meditates the way,
By force to ravish, or by fraud betray;
For when success a lover's toil attends,
Few ask if fraud or force attained his ends.
    For this, ere Phœbus rose, he had implored          35
Propitious heaven, and every power adored,
But chiefly Love – to Love an altar built
Of twelve vast French romances, neatly gilt.
There lay three garters, half a pair of gloves,
And all the trophies of his former loves.          40
With tender billet-doux he lights the pyre,
And breathes three amorous sighs to raise the fire;
Then prostrate falls, and begs with ardent eyes

Soon to obtain, and long possess, the prize.
The powers gave ear and granted half his prayer;          45
The rest, the winds dispersed in empty air.
    But now secure the painted vessel glides,
The sunbeams trembling on the floating tides,
While melting music steals upon the sky,
And softened sounds along the waters die:          50
Smooth flow the waves, the zephyrs gently play,
Belinda smiled, and all the world was gay.
All but the sylph – with careful thoughts oppressed,
The impending woe sat heavy on his breast.
He summons straight his denizens of air;          55
The lucid squadrons round the sails repair:
Soft o'er the shrouds aërial whispers breathe,
That seemed but zephyrs to the train beneath.
Some to the sun their insect-wings unfold,
Waft on the breeze, or sink in clouds of gold –          60
Transparent forms, too fine for mortal sight,
Their fluid bodies half dissolved in light.
Loose to the wind their airy garments flew,
Thin glittering textures of the filmy dew,
Dipped in the richest tincture of the skies,          65
Where light disports in ever-mingling dyes,
While every beam new transient colours flings –
Colours that change whene'er they wave their wings.
Amid the circle, on the gilded mast,
Superior by the head, was Ariel placed:          70
His purple pinions opening to the sun,
He raised his azure wand, and thus begun:
    'Ye sylphs and sylphids, to your chief give ear,
Fays, fairies, genii, elves, and dæmons hear!
Ye know the spheres and various tasks assigned          75
By laws eternal to the aërial kind:
Some in the fields of purest ether play,
And bask and whiten in the blaze of day;
Some guide the course of wandering orbs on high,
Or roll the planets through the boundless sky.          80
Some, less refined, beneath the moon's pale light
Pursue the stars that shoot athwart the night,
Or suck the mists in grosser air below,

Or dip their pinions in the painted bow,
Or brew fierce tempests on the wintry main,          85
Or o'er the glebe distil the kindly rain.
Others on earth o'er human race preside,
Watch all their ways, and all their actions guide:
Of these the chief the care of nations own,
And guard with arms divine the British throne.          90
   Our humbler province is to tend the fair –
Not a less pleasing (though less glorious) care;
To save the powder from too rude a gale,
Nor let the imprisoned essences exhale;
To draw fresh colours from the vernal flowers;          95
To steal from rainbows, e'er they drop in showers,
A brighter wash; to curl their waving hairs,
Assist their blushes, and inspire their airs.
Nay, oft, in dreams, invention we bestow,
To change a flounce, or add a furbelow.          100
   This day, black omens threat the brightest fair
That e'er deserved a watchful spirit's care –
Some dire disaster, or by force, or sleight:
But what, or where, the Fates have wrapped in night.
Whether the nymph shall break Diana's law,          105
Or some frail china jar receive a flaw;
Or stain her honour, or her new brocade,
Forget her prayers, or miss a masquerade,
Or lose her heart or necklace at a ball;
Or whether heaven has doomed that Shock must fall.          110
Haste then, ye spirits! To your charge repair:
The fluttering fan be Zephyretta's care;
The drops to thee, Brillante, we consign;
And, Momentilla, let the watch be thine;
Do thou, Crispissa, tend her favourite lock;          115
Ariel himself shall be the guard of Shock.
   To fifty chosen sylphs of special note
We trust the important charge, the petticoat.
Oft have we known that sevenfold fence to fail,
Though stiff with hoops and armed with ribs of whale:          120
Form a strong line about the silver bound,
And guard the wide circumference around.
   Whatever spirit, careless of his charge,

His post neglects, or leaves the fair at large,
Shall feel sharp vengeance soon o'ertake his sins,          125
Be stopped in vials, or transfixed with pins,
Or plunged in lakes of bitter washes lie,
Or wedged whole ages in a bodkin's eye:
Gums and pomatums shall his flight restrain,
While clogged he beats his silken wings in vain,            130
Or alum styptics, with contracting power,
Shrink his thin essence like a rivelled flower;
Or, as Ixion fixed, the wretch shall feel
The giddy motion of the whirling mill –
In fumes of burning chocolate shall glow,                   135
And tremble at the sea that froths below!'
   He spoke; the spirits from the sails descend;
Some, orb in orb, around the nymph extend,
Some thread the mazy ringlets of her hair,
Some hang upon the pendants of her ear;                     140
With beating hearts the dire event they wait,
Anxious, and trembling for the birth of Fate.


CANTO 3

Close by those meads, for ever crowned with flowers,
Where Thames with pride surveys his rising towers,
There stands a structure of majestic frame
Which from the neighbouring Hampton takes its name.
Here Britain's statesmen oft the fall foredoom             5
Of foreign tyrants, and of nymphs at home;
Here thou, great Anna, whom three realms obey,
Dost sometimes counsel take – and sometimes tea.
   Hither the heroes and the nymphs resort
To taste awhile the pleasures of a court;                  10
In various talk the instructive hours they passed –
Who gave the ball, or paid the visit last.
One speaks the glory of the British Queen,
And one describes a charming Indian screen;
A third interprets motions, looks, and eyes;               15
At every word a reputation dies.
Snuff, or the fan, supply each pause of chat,
With singing, laughing, ogling, and all that.

Meanwhile, declining from the noon of day,
The sun obliquely shoots his burning ray;                    20
The hungry judges soon the sentence sign,
And wretches hang that jurymen may dine;
The merchant from th'Exchange returns in peace,
And the long labours of the toilette cease.
Belinda now, whom thirst of fame invites,                    25
Burns to encounter two adventrous knights,
At ombre singly to decide their doom,
And swells her breast with conquests yet to come.
Straight the three bands prepare in arms to join,
Each band the number of the sacred nine.                    30
Soon as she spreads her hand, the aërial guard
Descend, and sit on each important card:
First Ariel perched upon a matador,
Then each, according to the rank they bore;
For sylphs, yet mindful of their ancient race,               35
Are, as when women, wondrous fond of place.
   Behold, four kings in majesty revered,
With hoary whiskers and a forky beard;
And four fair queens, whose hands sustain a flower,
Th'expressive emblem of their softer power;                  40
Four knaves in garbs succinct, a trusty band,
Caps on their heads, and halberds in their hand;
And particoloured troops – a shining train –
Draw forth to combat on the velvet plain.
   The skilful nymph reviews her force with care:            45
'Let spades be trumps!' she said, and trumps they were.
   Now move to war her sable matadors,
In show like leaders of the swarthy Moors:
Spadillio first, unconquerable lord,
Led off two captive trumps, and swept the board.            50
As many more Manillio forced to yield,
And marched a victor from the verdant field.
Him Basto followed, but his fate more hard
Gained but one trump, and one plebeian card.
With his broad sabre next, a chief in years,               55
The hoary majesty of spades appears,
Puts forth one manly leg, to sight revealed
(The rest, his many-coloured robe concealed).

The rebel knave, who dares his prince engage,
Proves the just victim of his royal rage.                                60
Even mighty Pam that kings and queens o'erthrew,
And mowed down armies in the fights of loo –
Sad chance of war – now, destitute of aid,
Falls undistinguished by the victor spade!
 Thus far both armies to Belinda yield;                        65
Now to the baron Fate inclines the field.
His warlike Amazon her host invades,
The imperial consort of the crown of spades.
The club's black tyrant first her victim died,
Spite of his haughty mien and barbarous pride:               70
What boots the regal circle on his head;
His giant limbs, in state unwieldy spread;
That long behind he trails his pompous robe,
And, of all monarchs, only grasps the globe?
 The baron now his diamonds pours apace:               75
Th' embroidered king, who shows but half his face,
And his refulgent queen, with powers combined,
Of broken troops an easy conquest find.
Clubs, diamonds, hearts, in wild disorder seen,
With throngs promiscuous strew the level green.              80
Thus, when dispersed, a routed army runs
Of Asia's troops, and Afric's sable sons;
With like confusion different nations fly,
Of various habit and of various dye:
The pierced battalions disunited fall                                85
In heaps on heaps: one fate o'erwhelms them all.
 The knave of diamonds tries his wily arts,
And wins (oh shameful chance!) the queen of hearts.
At this, the blood the virgin's cheek forsook,
A livid paleness spreads o'er all her look;                         90
She sees, and trembles at the approaching ill,
Just in the jaws of ruin, and codille.
And now (as oft in some distempered state)
On one nice trick depends the general fate.
An ace of hearts steps forth: the king, unseen,             95
Lurked in her hand, and mourned his captive queen:
He springs to vengeance with an eager pace,
And falls like thunder on the prostrate ace.

The nymph exulting fills with shouts the sky;
The walls, the woods, and long canals reply.          100
   Oh thoughtless mortals, ever blind to Fate,
Too soon dejected, and too soon elate!
Sudden these honours shall be snatched away,
And cursed for ever this victorious day.
   For lo, the board with cups and spoons is crowned,          105
The berries crackle, and the mill turns round;
On shining altars of japan they raise
The silver lamp; the fiery spirits blaze.
From silver spouts the grateful liquors glide,
While China's earth receives the smoking tide:          110
At once they gratify their scent and taste,
And frequent cups prolong the rich repast.
Straight hover round the fair her airy band:
Some, as she sipped, the fuming liquor fanned,
Some o'er her lap their careful plumes displayed,          115
Trembling, and conscious of the rich brocade.
Coffee (which makes the politician wise,
And see through all things with his half-shut eyes)
Sent up in vapours to the baron's brain
New stratagems the radiant lock to gain.          120
Ah cease, rash youth! Desist ere 'tis too late;
Fear the just gods, and think of Scylla's fate:
Changed to a bird, and sent to flit in air,
She dearly pays for Nisus' injured hair!
   But when to mischief mortals bend their will,          125
How soon they find fit instruments of ill!
Just then, Clarissa drew with tempting grace
A two-edged weapon from her shining case:
So ladies in romance assist their knight,
Present the spear, and arm him for the fight.          130
He takes the gift with reverence, and extends
The little engine on his fingers' ends.
This just behind Belinda's neck he spread,
As o'er the fragrant steams she bends her head.
Swift to the lock a thousand sprites repair,          135
A thousand wings, by turns, blow back the hair,
And thrice they twitched the diamond in her ear:
Thrice she looked back, and thrice the foe drew near.

Just in that instant, anxious Ariel sought
The close recesses of the virgin's thought:                               140
As on the nosegay in her breast reclined
He watched the ideas rising in her mind,
Sudden he viewed, in spite of all her art,
An earthly lover lurking at her heart.
Amazed, confused, he found his power expired,                             145
Resigned to Fate, and with a sigh retired.
    The peer now spreads the glittering forfex wide
To enclose the lock; now joins it, to divide.
Even then, before the fatal engine closed,
A wretched sylph too fondly interposed:                                   150
Fate urged the sheers and cut the sylph in twain
(But airy substance soon unites again);
The meeting points the sacred hair dissever
From the fair head for ever and for ever!
    Then flashed the living lightning from her eyes,                      155
And screams of horror rend the affrighted skies.
Not louder shrieks to pitying heaven are cast
When husbands, or when lapdogs, breathe their last,
Or when rich china vessels, fallen from high,
In glittering dust and painted fragments lie!                            160
    'Let wreaths of triumph now my temples twine'
(The victor cried), 'the glorious prize is mine!
While fish in streams, or birds delight in air,
Or in a coach and six the British fair,
As long as *Atalantis* shall be read,                                     165
Or the small pillow grace a lady's bed;
While visits shall be paid on solemn days
When numerous wax-lights in bright order blaze,
While nymphs take treats, or assignations give,
So long my honour, name, and praise shall live!                          170
What Time would spare, from steel receives its date,
And monuments, like men, submit to fate!
Steel could the labour of the gods destroy,
And strike to dust the imperial towers of Troy;
Steel could the works of mortal pride confound,                          175
And hew triumphal arches to the ground.
What wonder, then, fair nymph, thy hairs should feel
The conquering force of unresisted steel?'

## CANTO 4

But anxious cares the pensive nymph oppressed,
And secret passions laboured in her breast.
Not youthful kings in battle seized alive,
Not scornful virgins who their charms survive,
Not ardent lovers robbed of all their bliss,                    5
Not ancient ladies when refused a kiss,
Not tyrants fierce that unrepenting die,
Not Cynthia when her manteau's pinned awry,
E'er felt such rage, resentment, and despair,
As thou, sad virgin, for thy ravished hair!                     10
    For, that sad moment, when the sylphs withdrew,
And Ariel weeping from Belinda flew,
Umbriel, a dusky, melancholy sprite
As ever sullied the fair face of light,
Down to the central earth, his proper scene,                    15
Repaired to search the gloomy Cave of Spleen.
    Swift on his sooty pinions flits the gnome,
And in a vapour reached the dismal dome.
No cheerful breeze this sullen region knows –
The dreaded east is all the wind that blows.                    20
Here in a grotto, sheltered close from air,
And screened in shades from day's detested glare,
She sighs for ever on her pensive bed,
Pain at her side, and Megrim at her head.
    Two handmaids wait the throne, alike in place,              25
But differing far in figure and in face.
Here stood Ill-nature like an ancient maid,
Her wrinkled form in black and white arrayed:
With store of prayers for mornings, nights, and noons,
Her hand is filled; her bosom with lampoons.                    30
    There Affectation, with a sickly mien,
Shows in her cheek the roses of eighteen,
Practised to lisp and hang the head aside,
Faints into airs, and languishes with pride,
On the rich quilt sinks with becoming woe,                      35
Wrapped in a gown for sickness and for show.
The fair ones feel such maladies as these
When each new night-dress gives a new disease.

A constant vapour o'er the palace flies,
Strange phantoms rising as the mists arise, 40
Dreadful as hermit's dreams in haunted shades,
Or bright as visions of expiring maids:
Now glaring fiends, and snakes on rolling spires,
Pale spectres, gaping tombs, and purple fires;
Now lakes of liquid gold, Elysian scenes, 45
And crystal domes, and angels in machines.
Unnumbered throngs on every side are seen,
Of bodies changed to various forms by Spleen.
Here living teapots stand, one arm held out,
One bent; the handle this, and that the spout: 50
A pipkin there like Homer's tripod walks;
Here sighs a jar, and there a goose-pie talks;
Men prove with child as powerful fancy works,
And maids, turned bottles, call aloud for corks.
Safe passed the gnome through this fantastic band, 55
A branch of healing spleenwort in his hand,
Then thus addressed the power: 'Hail, wayward queen,
Who rule the sex to fifty from fifteen:
Parent of vapours and of female wit,
Who give the hysteric or poetic fit, 60
On various tempers act by various ways,
Make some take physic, others scribble plays;
Who cause the proud their visits to delay,
And send the godly in a pet to pray:
A nymph there is that all thy power disdains, 65
And thousands more in equal mirth maintains.
But oh, if e'er thy gnome could spoil a grace,
Or raise a pimple on a beauteous face,
Like citron-waters matrons' cheeks inflame,
Or change complexions at a losing game; 70
If e'er with airy horns I planted heads,
Or rumpled petticoats, or tumbled beds,
Or caused suspicion when no soul was rude,
Or discomposed the head-dress of a prude,
Or e'er to costive lap-dog gave disease, 75
Which not the tears of brightest eyes could ease:
Hear me, and touch Belinda with chagrin;
That single act gives half the world the spleen.'

The goddess with a discontented air
Seems to reject him, though she grants his prayer.                    80
A wondrous bag with both her hands she binds,
Like that where once Ulysses held the winds:
There she collects the force of female lungs,
Sighs, sobs, and passions, and the war of tongues.
A vial next she fills with fainting fears,                    85
Soft sorrows, melting griefs, and flowing tears.
The gnome, rejoicing, bears her gifts away,
Spreads his black wings, and slowly mounts to day.
    Sunk in Thalestris' arms the nymph he found,
Her eyes dejected and her hair unbound.                    90
Full o'er their heads the swelling bag he rent,
And all the furies issued at the vent.
Belinda burns with more than mortal ire,
And fierce Thalestris fans the rising fire.
'Oh wretched maid!' she spread her hands, and cried                    95
(While Hampton's echoes 'wretched maid' replied);
'Was it for this you took such constant care
The bodkin, comb, and essence to prepare?
For this your locks in paper durance bound,
For this with torturing irons wreathed around?                    100
For this with fillets strained your tender head,
And bravely bore the double loads of lead?
Gods! shall the ravisher display your hair,
While the fops envy, and the ladies stare!
Honour forbid, at whose unrivalled shrine                    105
Ease, pleasure, virtue, all, our sex resign.
Methinks already I your tears survey,
Already hear the horrid things they say,
Already see you a degraded toast,
And all your honour in a whisper lost!                    110
How shall I, then, your helpless fame defend?
'Twill then be infamy to seem your friend!
And shall this prize – the inestimable prize –
Exposed through crystal to the gazing eyes,
And heightened by the diamond's circling rays,                    115
On that rapacious hand for ever blaze?
Sooner shall grass in Hyde Park Circus grow,
And wits take lodgings in the sound of Bow;

Sooner let earth, air, sea, to chaos fall,
Men, monkeys, lap-dogs, parrots, perish all!'　　120
　She said; then raging to Sir Plume repairs,
And bids her beau demand the precious hairs
(Sir Plume of amber snuffbox justly vain
And the nice conduct of a clouded cane).
With earnest eyes and round unthinking face,　　125
He first the snuffbox opened, then the case,
And thus broke out: 'My lord, why, what the devil?
Zounds! Damn the lock! 'Fore Gad, you must be civil!
Plague on't! 'Tis past a jest – nay prithee, pox!
Give her the hair' – he spoke, and rapped his box.　　130
　'It grieves me much' (replied the peer again)
'Who speaks so well should ever speak in vain.
But by this lock – this sacred lock – I swear
(Which never more shall join its parted hair;
Which never more its honours shall renew,　　135
Clipped from the lovely head where late it grew)
That while my nostrils draw the vital air,
This hand, which won it, shall for ever wear.'
He spoke and, speaking, in proud triumph spread
The long-contended honours of her head.　　140
　But Umbriel, hateful gnome, forbears not so:
He breaks the vial whence the sorrows flow.
Then see, the nymph in beauteous grief appears,
Her eyes half-languishing, half-drowned in tears:
On her heaved bosom hung her drooping head,　　145
Which, with a sigh, she raised, and thus she said:
'For ever cursed be this detested day,
Which snatched my best, my favourite curl away!
Happy, ah ten times happy, had I been
If Hampton Court these eyes had never seen!　　150
Yet am not I the first mistaken maid
By love of courts to numerous ills betrayed.
Oh, had I rather unadmired remained
In some lone isle, or distant northern land,
Where the gilt chariot never marks the way,　　155
Where none learn ombre, none e'er taste bohea!
There kept my charms concealed from mortal eye,
Like roses that in deserts bloom and die.

What moved my mind with youthful lords to roam?
Oh had I stayed and said my prayers at home!          160
'Twas this the morning omens seemed to tell:
Thrice from my trembling hand the patch-box fell;
The tottering china shook without a wind;
Nay, Poll sat mute, and Shock was most unkind!
A sylph, too, warned me of the threats of Fate,          165
In mystic visions, now believed too late!
See the poor remnants of these slighted hairs –
My hands shall rend what even thy rapine spares.
These, in two sable ringlets taught to break,
Once gave new beauties to the snowy neck;          170
The sister-lock now sits uncouth, alone,
And in its fellow's fate foresees its own;
Uncurled it hangs, the fatal sheers demands,
And tempts once more thy sacrilegious hands.
Oh hadst thou, cruel, been content to seize          175
Hairs less in sight, or any hairs but these!'


## CANTO 5

She said: the pitying audience melt in tears,
But Fate and Jove had stopped the baron's ears.
In vain Thalestris with reproach assails,
For who can move when fair Belinda fails?
Not half so fixed the Trojan could remain,          5
While Anna begged and Dido raged in vain.
Then grave Clarissa graceful waved her fan,
Silence ensued, and thus the nymph began:
    'Say, why are beauties praised and honoured most,
The wise man's passion, and the vain man's toast?          10
Why decked with all that land and sea afford,
Why angels called, and angel-like adored?
Why round our coaches crowd the white-gloved beaus,
Why bows the side-box from its inmost rows?
How vain are all these glories, all our pains,          15
Unless good sense preserve what beauty gains:
That men may say, when we the front-box grace,
Behold the first in virtue as in face!
Oh, if to dance all night and dress all day

Charmed the smallpox, or chased old age away, 20
Who would not scorn what housewife's cares produce,
Or who would learn one earthly thing of use?
To patch, nay ogle, might become a saint,
Nor could it, sure, be such a sin to paint.
But since, alas, frail beauty must decay, 25
Curled or uncurled since locks will turn to grey;
Since painted, or not painted, all shall fade,
And she who scorns a man must die a maid,
What then remains but well our power to use,
And keep good humour still whate'er we lose? 30
And trust me, dear, good humour can prevail
When airs, and flights, and screams, and scolding fail.
Beauties in vain their pretty eyes may roll;
Charms strike the sight, but merit wins the soul.'
    So spoke the dame, but no applause ensued; 35
Belinda frowned, Thalestris called her prude.
'To arms, to arms!' the fierce virago cries,
And swift as lightning to the combat flies.
All side in parties and begin the attack:
Fans clap, silks rustle and tough whalebones crack; 40
Heroes' and heroines' shouts confusedly rise,
And bass and treble voices strike the skies.
No common weapons in their hands are found,
Like gods they fight, nor dread a mortal wound.
    So when bold Homer makes the gods engage, 45
And heavenly breasts with human passions rage,
'Gainst Pallas, Mars; Latona, Hermes arms,
And all Olympus rings with loud alarms.
Jove's thunder roars, heaven trembles all around,
Blue Neptune storms, the bellowing deeps resound: 50
Earth shakes her nodding towers, the ground gives way,
And the pale ghosts start at the flash of day!
    Triumphant Umbriel, on a sconce's height,
Clapped his glad wings, and sat to view the fight:
Propped on their bodkin spears the sprites survey 55
The growing combat, or assist the fray.
    While through the press enraged Thalestris flies,
And scatters deaths around from both her eyes,
A beau and witling perished in the throng,

One died in metaphor, and one in song.          60
'Oh cruel nymph, a living death I bear,'
Cried Dapperwit, and sunk beside his chair;
A mournful glance Sir Fopling upwards cast:
'Those eyes are made so killing' was his last.
Thus on Meander's flowery margin lies          65
Th' expiring swan, and as he sings he dies.
    When bold Sir Plume had drawn Clarissa down,
Chloe stepped in, and killed him with a frown;
She smiled to see the doughty hero slain,
But, at her smile, the beau revived again.          70
    Now Jove suspends his golden scales in air,
Weighs the men's wits against the lady's hair;
The doubtful beam long nods from side to side;
At length the wits mount up, the hairs subside.
    See fierce Belinda on the baron flies,          75
With more than usual lightning in her eyes:
Nor feared the chief the unequal fight to try,
Who sought no more than on his foe to die.
But this bold lord, with manly strength endued,
She with one finger and a thumb subdued:          80
Just where the breath of life his nostrils drew,
A charge of snuff the wily virgin threw:
The gnomes direct, to every atom just,
The pungent grains of titillating dust.
Sudden, with starting tears each eye o'erflows,          85
And the high dome re-echoes to his nose.
'Now meet thy fate,' incensed Belinda cried,
And drew a deadly bodkin from her side
(The same, his ancient personage to deck,
Her great great grandsire wore about his neck          90
In three seal-rings, which after, melted down,
Formed a vast buckle for his widow's gown:
Her infant grandame's whistle next it grew,
The bells she jingled, and the whistle blew;
Then in a bodkin graced her mother's hairs,          95
Which long she wore, and now Belinda wears).
    'Boast not my fall' (he cried) 'insulting foe!
Thou by some other shalt be laid as low.
Nor think, to die dejects my lofty mind:

All that I dread is leaving you behind!                    100
Rather than so, ah, let me still survive,
And burn in Cupid's flames – but burn alive.'
     'Restore the lock!' she cries, and all around
'Restore the lock!' the vaulted roofs rebound.
Not fierce Othello in so loud a strain                    105
Roared for the handkerchief that caused his pain.
But see how oft ambitious aims are crossed,
And chiefs contend 'till all the prize is lost!
The lock, obtained with guilt, and kept with pain,
In every place is sought, but sought in vain:              110
With such a prize no mortal must be blessed:
So heaven decrees – with heaven who can contest?
     Some thought it mounted to the lunar sphere,
Since all things lost on earth are treasured there.
There heroes' wits are kept in ponderous vases,           115
And beaus in snuffboxes and tweezer-cases.
There broken vows, and death-bed alms are found,
And lovers' hearts with ends of ribband bound,
The courtier's promises, and sick man's prayers,
The smiles of harlots, and the tears of heirs,            120
Cages for gnats, and chains to yoke a flea,
Dried butterflies, and tomes of casuistry.
     But trust the Muse – she saw it upward rise,
Though marked by none but quick, poetic eyes
(So Rome's great founder to the heavens withdrew,         125
To Proculus alone confessed in view):
A sudden star, it shot through liquid air,
And drew behind a radiant trail of hair.
Not Berenice's lock first rose so bright,
The heavens bespangling with dishevelled light.           130
The sylphs behold it kindling as it flies,
And pleased pursue its progress through the skies.
     This the beau monde shall from the Mall survey,
And hail with music its propitious ray.
This the blessed lover shall for Venus take,              135
And send up vows from Rosamonda's lake.
This Partridge soon shall view in cloudless skies,
When next he looks through Galileo's eyes;
And hence th' egregious wizard shall foredoom

The fate of Louis, and the fall of Rome.                                  140
    Then cease, bright nymph, to mourn thy ravished hair,
Which adds new glory to the shining sphere!
Not all the tresses that fair head can boast
Shall draw such envy as the lock you lost.
For, after all the murders of your eye,                                   145
When, after millions slain, yourself shall die;
When those fair suns shall set, as set they must,
And all those tresses shall be laid in dust,
This lock the Muse shall consecrate to fame,
And 'midst the stars inscribe Belinda's name.                            150

# Eloisa to Abelard

In these deep solitudes and awful cells,
Where heavenly-pensive Contemplation dwells,
And ever-musing Melancholy reigns,
What means this tumult in a vestal's veins?
Why rove my thoughts beyond this last retreat?      5
Why feels my heart its long-forgotten heat?
Yet, yet I love! – From Abelard it came,
And Eloisa yet must kiss the name.
　　Dear fatal name, rest ever unrevealed,
Nor pass these lips in holy silence sealed.      10
Hide it, my heart, within that close disguise,
Where, mixed with God's, his loved idea lies.
Oh write it not, my hand – the name appears
Already written – wash it out, my tears!
In vain lost Eloisa weeps and prays,      15
Her heart still dictates, and her hand obeys.
　　Relentless walls, whose darksome round contains
Repentant sighs and voluntary pains;
Ye rugged rocks, which holy knees have worn;
Ye grots and caverns shagged with horrid thorn!      20
Shrines, where their vigils pale-eyed virgins keep,
And pitying saints, whose statues learn to weep!
Though cold like you, unmoved and silent grown,
I have not yet forgot myelf to stone.
All is not heaven's while Abelard has part –      25
Still rebel nature holds out half my heart;
Nor prayers nor fasts its stubborn pulse restrain,
Nor tears, for ages taught to flow in vain.
　　Soon as thy letters, trembling, I unclose,
That well-known name awakens all my woes:      30
Oh name for ever sad, for ever dear,
Still breathed in sighs, still ushered with a tear!
I tremble, too, where'er my own I find –
Some dire misfortune follows close behind.
Line after line my gushing eyes o'erflow,      35

Led through a sad variety of woe:
Now warm in love, now withering in thy bloom,
Lost in a convent's solitary gloom!
There stern religion quenched the unwilling flame,
There died the best of passions, love and fame.                    40
    Yet write, oh write me all, that I may join
Griefs to thy griefs, and echo sighs to thine:
Nor foes nor fortune take this power away;
And is my Abelard less kind than they?
Tears still are mine, and those I need not spare,                   45
Love but demands what else were shed in prayer;
No happier task these faded eyes pursue:
To read and weep is all they now can do.
    Then share thy pain, allow that sad relief:
Ah, more than share it – give me all thy grief!                    50
Heaven first taught letters for some wretch's aid,
Some banished lover, or some captive maid;
They live, they speak, they breathe what love inspires,
Warm from the soul, and faithful to its fires.
The virgin's wish without her fears impart,                        55
Excuse the blush, and pour out all the heart,
Speed the soft intercourse from soul to soul,
And waft a sigh from Indus to the Pole.
    Thou knowest how guiltless first I met thy flame,
When love approachd me under friendship's name;                    60
My fancy formed thee of angelic kind,
Some emanation of the all-beauteous Mind.
Those smiling eyes, attempering every ray,
Shone sweetly lambent with celestial day:
Guiltless I gazed, heaven listened while you sung,                 65
And truths divine came mended from that tongue.
From lips like those what precept failed to move?
Too soon they taught me 'twas no sin to love.
Back through the paths of pleasing sense I ran,
Nor wished an angel whom I loved a man.                            70
Dim and remote the joys of saints I see,
Nor envy them that heaven I lose for thee.
    How oft, when pressed to marriage, have I said,
Curse on all laws but those which love has made!
Love, free as air, at sight of human ties                         75

Spreads his light wings, and in a moment flies.
Let wealth, let honour, wait the wedded dame,
August her deed, and sacred be her fame;
Before true passion all those views remove –
Fame, wealth, and honour: what are you to Love?               80
The jealous god, when we profane his fires,
Those restless passions in revenge inspires,
And bids them make mistaken mortals groan,
Who seek in love for aught but love alone.
Should at my feet the world's great master fall,              85
Himself, his throne, his world, I'd scorn 'em all:
Nor Cæsar's empress would I deign to prove;
No, make me mistress to the man I love.
If there be yet another name more free,
More fond, than mistress, make me that to thee!               90
Oh happy state, when souls each other draw,
When love is liberty, and nature, law:
All then is full, possessing, and possessed,
No craving void left aching in the breast:
Even thought meets thought ere from the lips it part,         95
And each warm wish springs mutual from the heart.
This sure is bliss (if bliss on earth there be),
And once the lot of Abelard and me.
    Alas, how changed! What sudden horrors rise!
A naked lover bound and bleeding lies!                        100
Where, where was Eloise – her voice, her hand,
Her poniard, had opposed the dire command.
Barbarian, stay! That bloody stroke restrain!
The crime was common, common be the pain.
I can no more; by shame, by rage suppressed,                  105
Let tears and burning blushes speak the rest.
    Canst thou forget that sad, that solemn day,
When victims at yon altar's foot we lay?
Canst thou forget what tears that moment fell
When, warm in youth, I bade the world farewell?              110
As with cold lips I kissed the sacred veil,
The shrines all trembled, and the lamps grew pale:
Heaven scarce believed the conquest it surveyed,
And saints with wonder heard the vows I made.
Yet then, to those dread altars as I drew,                    115

Not on the cross my eyes were fixed, but you;
Not grace, or zeal – love only was my call,
And if I lose thy love, I lose my all.
Come! With thy looks, thy words, relieve my woe;
Those still at least are left thee to bestow.                    120
Still on that breast enamoured let me lie,
Still drink delicious poison from thy eye,
Pant on thy lip, and to thy heart be pressed:
Give all thou canst, and let me dream the rest.
Ah no! Instruct me other joys to prize,                         125
With other beauties charm my partial eyes;
Full in my view set all the bright abode,
And make my soul quit Abelard for God.
    Ah, think at least thy flock deserve thy care,
Plants of thy hand, and children of thy prayer.                 130
From the false world in early youth they fled,
By thee to mountains, wilds, and deserts led.
You raised these hallowed walls, the desert smiled,
And paradise was opened in the wild.
No weeping orphan saw his father's stores                       135
Our shrines irradiate, or emblaze the floors;
No silver saints, by dying misers given,
Here bribed the rage of ill-requited heaven,
But such plain roofs as piety could raise,
And only vocal with the Maker's praise.                         140
In these lone walls (their days eternal bound),
These moss-grown domes with spiry turrets crowned,
Where awful arches make a noon-day night.
And the dim windows shed a solemn light,
Thy eyes diffused a reconciling ray,                            145
And gleams of glory brightened all the day.
But now no face divine contentment wears;
'Tis all blank sadness, or continual tears.
See how the force of others' prayers I try
(Oh pious fraud of amorous charity!) –                          150
But why should I on others' prayers depend?
Come thou, my father, brother, husband, friend!
Ah, let thy handmaid, sister, daughter move,
And all those tender names in one, thy love!
The darksome pines that o'er yon rocks reclined                 155

Wave high, and murmur to the hollow wind;
The wandering streams that shine between the hills;
The grots that echo to the tinkling rills;
The dying gales that pant upon the trees;
The lakes that quiver to the curling breeze –                    160
No more these scenes my meditation aid,
Or lull to rest the visionary maid.
But o'er the twilight groves and dusky caves,
Long-sounding isles, and intermingled graves,
Black Melancholy sits, and round her throws                    165
A death-like silence, and a dread repose:
Her gloomy presence saddens all the scene,
Shades every flower, and darkens every green,
Deepens the murmur of the falling floods,
And breathes a browner horror on the woods.                    170
　　Yet here for ever, ever must I stay,
Sad proof how well a lover can obey!
Death, only death, can break the lasting chain,
And here, even then, shall my cold dust remain –
Here all its frailties, all its flames resign,                    175
And wait, till 'tis no sin to mix with thine.
　　Ah, wretch! Believed the spouse of God in vain,
Confessed within the slave of love and man.
Assist me, heaven! But whence arose that prayer?
Sprung it from piety, or from despair?                    180
Even here, where frozen chastity retires,
Love finds an altar for forbidden fires.
I ought to grieve, but cannot what I ought;
I mourn the lover, not lament the fault;
I view my crime, but kindle at the view;                    185
Repent old pleasures, and solicit new.
Now turned to heaven, I weep my past offence;
Now think of thee, and curse my innocence.
Of all affliction taught a lover yet,
'Tis sure the hardest science to forget!                    190
How shall I lose the sin, yet keep the sense,
And love the offender, yet detest the offence?
How the dear object from the crime remove,
Or how distinguish penitence from love?
Unequal task, a passion to resign,                    195

For hearts so touched, so pierced, so lost as mine.
Ere such a soul regains its peaceful state,
How often must it love, how often hate!
How often hope, despair, resent, regret,
Conceal, disdain – do all things but forget.                    200
But let heaven seize it, all at once 'tis fired;
Not touched, but raped; not wakened, but inspired!
Oh, come! Oh, teach me nature to subdue,
Renounce my love, my life, my self – and you.
Fill my fond heart with God alone, for he                       205
Alone can rival, can succeed to thee.
      How happy is the blameless vestal's lot,
The world forgetting, by the world forgot.
Eternal sunshine of the spotless mind;
Each prayer accepted, and each wish resigned;                   210
Labour and rest, that equal periods keep;
'Obedient slumbers that can wake and weep';
Desires composed, affections ever even;
Tears that delight, and sighs that waft to heaven.
Grace shines around her with serenest beams,                    215
And whispering angels prompt her golden dreams.
For her the unfading rose of Eden blooms,
And wings of seraphs shed divine perfumes;
For her the spouse prepares the bridal ring;
For her white virgins hymeneals sing:                           220
To sounds of heavenly harps she dies away,
And melts in visions of eternal day.
      Far other dreams my erring soul employ,
Far other raptures, of unholy joy:
When, at the close of each sad, sorrowing day,                  225
Fancy restores what vengeance snatched away,
Then conscience sleeps and, leaving nature free,
All my loose soul unbounded springs to thee.
Oh cursed, dear horrors of all-conscious night,
How glowing guilt exalts the keen delight!                      230
Provoking demons all restraint remove,
And stir within me every source of love.
I hear thee, view thee, gaze o'er all thy charms,
And round thy phantom glue my clasping arms.
I wake. No more I hear, no more I view –                        235

The phantom flies me, as unkind as you.
I call aloud; it hears not what I say.
I stretch my empty arms; it glides away.
To dream once more I close my willing eyes –
Ye soft illusions, dear deceits, arise!                    240
Alas, no more! Methinks we wandering go
Through dreary wastes, and weep each other's woe,
Where round some mouldering tower pale ivy creeps,
And low-browed rocks hang nodding o'er the deeps.
Sudden you mount; you beckon from the skies;              245
Clouds interpose, waves roar, and winds arise.
I shriek, start up, the same sad prospect find,
And wake to all the griefs I left behind.
    For thee the Fates, severely kind, ordain
A cool suspense from pleasure and from pain –            250
Thy life a long, dead calm of fixed repose;
No pulse that riots, and no blood that glows.
Still as the sea, ere winds were taught to blow,
Or moving spirit bade the waters flow;
Soft as the slumbers of a saint forgiven,                255
And mild as opening gleams of promised heaven.
    Come, Abelard, for what hast thou to dread?
The torch of Venus burns not for the dead.
Nature stands checked; Religion disapproves;
Even thou art cold – yet Eloisa loves.                    260
Ah hopeless, lasting flames, like those that burn
To light the dead, and warm the unfruitful urn!
    What scenes appear where'er I turn my view!
The dear ideas, where I fly, pursue,
Rise in the grove, before the altar rise,                255
Stain all my soul, and wanton in my eyes.
I waste the matin lamp in sighs for thee,
Thy image steals between my God and me,
Thy voice I seem in every hymn to hear,
With every bead I drop too soft a tear.                   270
When from the censer clouds of fragrance roll,
And swelling organs lift the rising soul,
One thought of thee puts all the pomp to flight –
Priests, tapers, temples, swim before my sight:
In seas of flame my plunging soul is drowned,            275

While altars blaze and angels tremble round.
    While prostrate here in humble grief I lie,
Kind, virtuous drops just gathering in my eye;
While praying, trembling, in the dust I roll,
And dawning grace is opening on my soul,                    280
Come, if thou darest, all charming as thou art!
Oppose thyself to heaven; dispute my heart.
Come – with one glance of those deluding eyes
Blot out each bright idea of the skies;
Take back that grace, those sorrows, and those tears,       285
Take back my fruitless penitence and prayers,
Snatch me, just mounting, from the blessed abode,
Assist the fiends, and tear me from my God!
    No, fly me, fly me, far as Pole from Pole;
Rise Alps between us, and whole oceans roll!                290
Ah, come not, write not, think not once of me,
Nor share one pang of all I felt for thee.
Thy oaths I quit, thy memory resign –
Forget, renounce me, hate whate'er was mine.
Fair eyes and tempting looks (which yet I view)             295
Long loved, adored ideas, all adieu!
Oh Grace serene; oh Virtue heavenly fair,
Divine oblivion of low-thoughted care!
Fresh blooming Hope, gay daughter of the sky!
And Faith, our early immortality!                           300
Enter, each mild, each amicable guest;
Receive, and wrap me in eternal rest!
    See in her cell sad Eloisa spread,
Propped on some tomb, a neighbour of the dead.
In each low wind methinks a spirit calls,                   305
And more than echoes talk along the walls.
Here, as I watched the dying lamps around,
From yonder shrine I heard a hollow sound.
'Come, sister, come!' (it said, or seemed to say)
'Thy place is here, sad sister come away!                   310
Once like thyself I trembled, wept, and prayed,
Love's victim then, though now a sainted maid.
But all is calm in this eternal sleep;
Here grief forgets to groan, and love to weep,
Even superstition loses every fear,                         315

For God, not man, absolves our frailties here.'
I come, I come! Prepare your roseate bowers,
Celestial palms, and ever-blooming flowers.
Thither, where sinners may have rest, I go,
Where flames refined in breasts seraphic glow.          320
Thou, Abelard, the last sad office pay,
And smooth my passage to the realms of day:
See my lips tremble, and my eyeballs roll,
Suck my last breath, and catch my flying soul!
Ah no – in sacred vestments mayest thou stand,          325
The hallowed taper trembling in thy hand,
Present the cross before my lifted eye,
Teach me at once, and learn of me to die.
Ah then, thy once-lovd Eloisa see:
It will be then no crime to gaze on me.                 330
See from my cheek the transient roses fly,
See the last sparkle languish in my eye,
Till every motion, pulse, and breath be o'er,
And even my Abelard beloved no more!
Oh Death all-eloquent, you only prove                   335
What dust we dote on when 'tis man we love!
Then, too, when Fate shall thy fair frame destroy
(That cause of all my guilt, and all my joy),
In trance ecstatic may thy pangs be drowned,
Bright clouds descend, and angels watch thee round;     340
From opening skies may streaming glories shine,
And saints embrace thee with a love like mine.
May one kind grave unite each hapless name,
And graft my love immortal on thy fame!
Then, ages hence, when all my woes are o'er,            345
When this rebellious heart shall beat no more,
If ever chance two wandering lovers brings
To Paraclete's white walls and silver springs,
O'er the pale marble shall they join their heads,
And drink the falling tears each other sheds;           350
Then sadly say, with mutual pity moved:
'Oh, may we never love as these have loved!'
From the full choir when loud hosannas rise,
And swell the pomp of dreadful sacrifice,
Amid that scene, if some relenting eye                  355

Glance on the stone where our cold relics lie,
Devotion's self shall steal a thought from heaven,
One human tear shall drop, and be forgiven.
And, sure, if Fate some future bard shall join
In sad similitude of griefs to mine,                          360
Condemned whole years in absence to deplore,
And image charms he must behold no more –
Such if there be, who loves so long, so well,
Let him our sad, our tender story tell:
The well-sung woes will sooth my pensive ghost;             365
He best can paint 'em who shall feel 'em most.

# Elegy

## To the Memory of an
## Unfortunate Lady

What beckoning ghost along the moonlit shade
Invites my step, and points to yonder glade?
'Tis she! – but why that bleeding bosom gored,
Why dimly gleams the visionary sword?
Oh, ever beauteous, ever friendly: tell,                         5
Is it, in heaven, a crime to love too well?
To bear too tender, or too firm a heart,
To act a lover's or a Roman's part?
Is there no bright reversion in the sky
For those who greatly think, or bravely die?                     10
    Why bade ye else, ye powers, her soul aspire
Above the vulgar flight of low desire?
Ambition first sprung from your blessed abodes,
The glorious fault of angels and of gods:
Thence to their images on earth it flows,                        15
And in the breasts of kings and heroes glows.
Most souls, 'tis true, but peep out once an age,
Dull sullen prisoners in the body's cage:
Dim lights of life, that burn a length of years,
Useless, unseen, as lamps in sepulchres:                         20
Like eastern kings a lazy state they keep,
And close confined in their own palace sleep.
    From these, perhaps (ere Nature bade her die),
Fate snatched her early to the pitying sky.
As into air the purer spirits flow,                              25
And separate from their kindred dregs below,
So flew the soul to its congenial place,
Nor left one virtue to redeem her race.
    But thou, false guardian of a charge too good;
Thou, mean deserter of thy brother's blood,                      30
See on these ruby lips the trembling breath,
These cheeks, now fading at the blast of death:
Cold is that breast which warmed the world before,

And those love-darting eyes must roll no more.
Thus, if eternal justice rules the ball,                                    35
Thus shall your wives, and thus your children fall:
On all the line a sudden vengeance waits,
And frequent hearses shall besiege your gates.
There passengers shall stand, and pointing say
(While the long funerals blacken all the way),                        40
'Lo, these were they, whose souls the Furies steeled,
And cursed with hearts unknowing how to yield.
Thus unlamented pass the proud away,
The gaze of fools, and pageant of a day!
So perish all, whose breast ne'er learned to glow            45
For others' good, or melt at others' woe.'
      What can atone (oh ever-injured shade!)
Thy fate unpitied, and thy rites unpaid?
No friend's complaint, no kind domestic tear
Pleased thy pale ghost, or graced thy mournful bier;        50
By foreign hands thy dying eyes were closed,
By foreign hands thy decent limbs composed,
By foreign hands thy humble grave adorned,
By strangers honoured, and by strangers mourned!
What though no friends in sable weeds appear,                55
Grieve for an hour, perhaps, then mourn a year,
And bear about the mockery of woe
To midnight dances, and the public show?
What though no weeping Loves thy ashes grace,
Nor polished marble emulate thy face?                              60
What though no sacred earth allow thee room,
Nor hallowed dirge be muttered o'er thy tomb?
Yet shall thy grave with rising flowers be dressed,
And the green turf lie lightly on thy breast:
There shall the morn her earliest tears bestow,              65
There the first roses of the year shall blow,
While angels with their silver wings o'ershade
The ground, now sacred by thy relics made.
      So peaceful rests, without a stone, a name,
What once had beauty, titles, wealth, and fame.            70
How loved, how honoured once, avails thee not,
To whom related, or by whom begot;
A heap of dust alone remains of thee:

'Tis all thou art, and all the proud shall be!
   Poets themselves must fall, like those they sung;     75
Deaf the praised ear, and mute the tuneful tongue.
Even he, whose soul now melts in mournful lays,
Shall shortly want the generous tear he pays;
Then from his closing eyes thy form shall part,
And the last pang shall tear thee from his heart,     80
Life's idle business at one gasp be o'er,
The Muse forgot, and thou beloved no more!

# Of Taste:
## An Epistle to the
## Right Honourable
## Richard, Earl of Burlington

'Tis strange the miser should his cares employ
To gain those riches he can ne'er enjoy.
Is it less strange the prodigal should waste
His wealth to purchase what he ne'er can taste?
Not for himself he sees, or hears, or eats:       5
Artists must choose his pictures, music, meats.
He buys for Topham drawings and designs,
For Pembroke statues, dirty gods, and coins;
Rare monkish manuscripts for Hearne alone,
And books for Mead, and butterflies for Sloane.      10
Think we all these are for himself? – no more
Than his fine wife, alas, or finer whore.
    For what has Virro painted, built, and planted?
Only to show how many tastes he wanted.
What brought Sir Visto's ill-got wealth to waste?      15
Some demon whispered, 'Visto! have a taste.'
Heaven visits with a taste the wealthy fool,
And needs no rod but Ripley with a rule.
See, sportive Fate, to punish awkward pride,
Bids Bubo build, and sends him such a guide:      20
A standing sermon, at each year's expense,
That never coxcomb reached magnificence!
    You show us Rome was glorious, not profuse,
And pompous buildings once were things of use.
Yet shall (my lord) your just, your noble rules      25
Fill half the land with imitating fools,
Who random drawings from your sheets shall take,
And of one beauty many blunders make;
Load some vain church with old theatric state,
Turn arcs of triumph to a garden gate;      30
Reverse your ornaments, and hang them all

On some patched dog-hole eked with ends of wall,
Then clap four slices of pilaster on it
That, laced with bits of rustic, makes a front;
Or call the winds through long arcades to roar,                    35
Proud to catch cold at a Venetian door;
Conscious they act a true Palladian part
And, if they starve, they starve by rules of art.
   Oft have you hinted, to your brother peer,
A certain truth, which many buy too dear:                          40
Something there is more needful than expense,
And something previous even to taste – 'tis sense:
Good sense, which only is the gift of heaven,
And, though no science, fairly worth the seven –
A light which in yourself you must perceive.                       45
Jones and Le Nôtre have it not to give.
   To build, to plant, whatever you intend,
To rear the column, or the arch to bend,
To swell the terrace or to sink the grot –
In all, let Nature never be forgot,                                50
But treat the goddess like a modest fair,
Nor overdress, nor leave her wholly bare;
Let not each beauty everywhere be spied,
Where half the skill is decently to hide.
He gains all points who pleasingly confounds,                      55
Surprises, varies, and conceals the bounds.
   Consult the genius of the place in all:
That tells the waters or to rise, or fall,
Or helps the ambitious hill the heavens to scale,
Or scoops in circling theatres the vale;                           60
Calls in the country, catches opening glades,
Joins willing woods, and varies shades from shades;
Now breaks, or now directs, the intending lines,
Paints as you plant and, as you work, designs.
   Still follow sense, of every art the soul,             65
Parts answering parts shall slide into a whole,
Spontaneous beauties all around advance,
Start even from difficulty, strike from chance:
Nature shall join you; Time shall make it grow
A Work to wonder at – perhaps a Stowe.                             70
   Without it, proud Versailles, thy glory falls,

And Nero's terraces desert their walls:
The vast parterres a thousand hands shall make,
Lo! Cobham comes, and floats them with a lake.
Or cut wide views through mountains to the plain,          75
You'll wish your hill or sheltered seat again.
Even in an ornament its place remark,
Nor in an Hermitage set Dr Clarke.

    Behold Villario's ten-years' toil complete –
His arbours darken, his espaliers meet;          80
The wood supports the plain, the parts unite;
And strength of shade contends with strength of light.
A waving glow the bloomy beds display,
Blushing in bright diversities of day,
With silver-quivering rills meandered o'er:          85
Enjoy them, you! Villario can no more;
Tired of the scene, parterres and fountains yield,
He finds at last he better likes a field.

    Through his young woods how pleased Sabinus strayed,
Or sat delighted in the thickening shade,          90
With annual joy the reddening shoots to greet,
Or see the stretching branches long to meet.
His son's fine taste an opener vista loves
(Foe to the dryads of his father's groves),
One boundless green, or flourished carpet, views,          95
With all the mournful family of yews;
The thriving plants, ignoble broomsticks made,
Now sweep those alleys they were born to shade.

    At Timon's villa let us pass a day,
Where all cry out, 'What sums are thrown away!'          100
So proud, so grand, of that stupendous air
Soft and agreeable come never there.
Greatness, with Timon, dwells in such a draught
As brings all Brobdignag before your thought.
To compass this, his building is a town,          105
His pond an ocean, his parterre a down:
Who but must laugh the master when he sees
A puny insect, shivering at a breeze!
Lo, what huge heaps of littleness around,
The whole, a laboured quarry above ground.          110
Two Cupids squirt before; a lake behind

Improves the keenness of the northern wind.
His gardens next your admiration call:
On every side you look, behold the wall!
No pleasing intricacies intervene,                           115
No artful wildness to perplex the scene;
Grove nods at grove, each alley has a brother,
And half the platform just reflects the other.
The suffering eye inverted nature sees,
Trees cut to statues, statues thick as trees,               120
With here a fountain never to be played,
And there a summer-house that knows no shade.
Here Amphitrite sails through myrtle bowers;
There gladiators fight, or die, in flowers;
Unwatered see the drooping sea-horse mourn,                 125
And swallows roost in Nilus' dusty urn.
    My lord advances with majestic mien,
Smit with the mighty pleasure, to be seen.
But soft – by regular approach – not yet –
First through the length of yon hot terrace sweat,          130
And when up ten steep slopes you've dragged your thighs,
Just at his study door he'll bless your eyes.
    His study! With what authors is it stored?
In books, not authors, curious is my lord:
To all their dated backs he turns you round –              135
These Aldus printed, those Du Suëil has bound.
Lo, some are vellum, and the rest as good
(For all his lordship knows) – but they are wood.
For Locke or Milton 'tis in vain to look,
These shelves admit not any modern book.                    140
    And now the chapel's silver bell you hear,
That summons you to all the pride of prayer:
Light quirks of music, broken and uneven,
Make the soul dance upon a jig to heaven.
On painted ceilings you devoutly stare,                     145
Where sprawl the saints of Verrio or Laguerre,
On gilded clouds in fair expansion lie,
And bring all paradise before your eye.
To rest, the cushion and soft dean invite,
Who never mentions hell to ears polite.                     150
    But hark! The chiming clocks to dinner call;

A hundred footsteps scrape the marble hall:
The rich buffet well-coloured serpents grace,
And gaping Tritons spew to wash your face.
Is this a dinner? This a genial room?                    155
No, 'tis a temple, and a hecatomb,
A solemn sacrifice, performed in state,
You drink by measure, and to minutes eat.
So quick retires each flying course, you'd swear
Sancho's dread doctor and his wand were there.           160
Between each act the trembling salvers ring,
From soup to sweet-wine, and God bless the king.
In plenty starving, tantalised in state,
And complaisantly helped to all I hate,
Treated, caressed, and tired, I take my leave,           165
Sick of his civil pride from morn to eve.
I curse such lavish cost and little skill,
And swear no day was ever passed so ill.
     Yet hence the poor are clothed, the hungry fed:
Health to himself, and to his infants bread              170
The labourer bears: what his hard heart denies,
His charitable vanity supplies.
     Another age shall see the golden ear
Embrown the slope, and nod on the parterre;
Deep harvests bury all his pride has planned,            175
And laughing Ceres reassume the land.
     Who then shall grace, or who improve the soil?
Who plants like Bathurst, or who builds like Boyle?
'Tis use alone that sanctifies expense,
And splendour borrows all her rays from sense.           180
     His father's acres who enjoys in peace,
Or makes his neighbours glad if he increase;
Whose cheerful tenants bless their yearly toil,
Yet to their lord owe more than to the soil;
Whose ample lawns are not ashamed to feed                185
The milky heifer and deserving steed;
Whose rising forests, not for pride or show,
But future buildings, future navies grow:
Let his plantations stretch from down to down,
First shade a country, and then raise a town.            190
     You too proceed! Make falling arts your care,

Erect new wonders, and the old repair.
Jones and Palladio to themselves restore,
And be whate'er Vitruvius was before:
Till kings call forth the ideas of your mind          195
(Proud to accomplish what such hands designed),
Bid harbours open, public ways extend,
Bid temples, worthier of the god, ascend,
Bid the broad arch the dangerous flood contain,
The mole projected break the roaring main;           200
Back to his bounds their subject sea command,
And roll obedient rivers through the land:
These honours, peace to happy Britain brings –
These are imperial works, and worthy kings.

# An Epistle from Mr Pope to Dr Arbuthnot

'Shut, shut the door, good John!' fatigued I said,
'Tie up the knocker, say I'm sick, I'm dead.
The dog-star rages! Nay, 'tis past a doubt,
All Bedlam, or Parnassus, is let out:
Fire in each eye, and papers in each hand,                    5
They rave, recite, and madden round the land.'
    What walls can guard me, or what shades can hide?
They pierce my thickets, through my grot they glide,
By land, by water, they renew the charge,
They stop the chariot, and they board the barge.             10
No place is sacred, not the church is free –
Even Sunday shines no sabbath day to me:
Then from the Mint walks forth the man of rhyme,
Happy to catch me, just at dinner-time.
    Is there a parson, much bemused in beer,                 15
A maudlin poetess, a rhyming peer,
A clerk, foredoomed his father's soul to cross,
Who pens a stanza, when he should engross?
Is there, who, locked from ink and paper, scrawls
With desperate charcoal round his darkened walls?            20
All fly to Twitnam and, in humble strain,
Apply to me to keep them mad or vain.
Arthur, whose giddy son neglects the laws,
Imputes to me and my damned works the cause:
Poor Cornus sees his frantic wife elope,                     25
And curses wit, and poetry, and Pope.
    Friend to my life (which, did not you prolong,
The world had wanted many an idle song)
What drop or nostrum can this plague remove?
Or which must end me, a fool's wrath or love?               30
A dire dilemma! Either way I'm sped –
If foes, they write, if friends, they read me dead.
Seized and tied down to judge, how wretched I,
Who can't be silent, and who will not lie:

To laugh were want of goodness and of grace,                    35
And to be grave exceeds all power of face.
I sit with sad civility; I read
With honest anguish and an aching head,
And drop at last, but in unwilling ears,
This saving counsel: 'Keep your piece nine years.'              40
   'Nine years!' cries he who, high in Drury Lane,
Lulled by soft zephyrs through the broken pane,
Rhymes ere he wakes, and prints before term ends,
Obliged by hunger and request of friends:
'The piece, you think, is incorrect? Why, take it,             45
I'm all submission, what you'd have it, make it.'
   Three things another's modest wishes bound –
My friendship, and a prologue, and ten pound.
   Pitholeon sends to me: 'You know his grace:
I want a patron – ask him for a place.'                        50
Pitholeon libelled me – 'but here's a letter
Informs you, sir, 'twas when he knew no better.
Dare you refuse him? Curll invites to dine,
He'll write a journal, or he'll turn divine.'
   Bless me, a packet – ''Tis a stranger sues,               55
A virgin tragedy, an orphan Muse.'
If I dislike it, 'Furies, death and rage!'
If I approve, 'Commend it to the stage.'
There (thank my stars) my whole commission ends –
The players and I are, luckily, no friends.                    60
Fired that the house reject him, ''Sdeath I'll print it,
And shame the fools – your interest, sir, with Lintot.'
Lintot, dull rogue, will think your price too much.
'Not, sir, if you revise it, and retouch.'
All my demurs but double his attacks;                          65
At last he whispers, 'Do, and we go snacks.'
Glad of a quarrel, straight I clap the door –
Sir, let me see your works and you no more.
   'Tis sung, when Midas' ears began to spring
(Midas, a sacred person and a king),                           70
His very minister who spied them first
(Some say his queen) was forced to speak, or burst.
And is not mine, my friend, a sorer case,
When every coxcomb perks them in my face?

'Good friend, forbear! You deal in dangerous things.          75
I'd never name queens, ministers, or kings;
Keep close to ears, and those let asses prick,
'Tis nothing' – Nothing? If they bite and kick?
Out with it, *Dunciad*: let the secret pass –
That secret to each fool – that he's an ass.          80
The truth once told (and wherefore should we lie?),
The queen of Midas slept, and so may I.
  You think this cruel? Take it for a rule,
No creature smarts so little as a fool.
Let peals of laughter, Codrus, round thee break:          85
Thou, unconcerned, canst hear the mighty crack:
Pit, box, and gallery in convulsions hurled,
Thou standest unshook amidst a bursting world.
Who shames a scribbler? Break one cobweb through,
He spins the slight, self-pleasing thread anew.          90
Destroy his fib or sophistry: in vain –
The creature's at his dirty work again,
Throned in the centre of his thin designs,
Proud of a vast extent of flimsy lines!
Whom have I hurt? Has poet yet, or seer,          95
Lost the arched eye-brow or Parnassian sneer?
And has not Colley still his lord, and whore?
His butchers Henley, his freemasons Moore?
Does not one table Bavius still admit?
Still to one bishop Philips seem a wit?          100
Still Sappho – 'Hold, for God's sake – you'll offend;
No names – be calm – learn prudence of a friend:
I too could write, and I am twice as tall –
But foes like these' – One flatterer's worse than all:
Of all mad creatures, if the learned are right,          105
It is the slaver kills, and not the bite.
A fool quite angry is quite innocent:
Alas! 'tis ten times worse when they *repent*.
  One dedicates in high heroic prose,
And ridicules beyond a hundred foes:          110
One from all Grub Street will my fame defend
And, more abusive, calls himself my friend.
This prints my letters, that expects a bribe,
And others roar aloud, 'Subscribe, subscribe.'

There are, who to my person pay their court:          115
I cough like Horace, and, though lean, am short:
'Ammon's great son one shoulder had too high;
Such Ovid's nose, and "Sir! you have an eye –".'
Go on, obliging creatures, make me see
All that disgraced my betters, met in me.          120
Say for my comfort, languishing in bed,
'Just so immortal Maro held his head.'
And when I die, be sure you let me know
'Great Homer died three thousand years ago.'
Why did I write? What sin to me unknown          125
Dipped me in ink, my parents', or my own?
As yet a child, nor yet a fool to fame,
I lisped in numbers, for the numbers came.
I left no calling for this idle trade,
No duty broke, no father disobeyed.          130
The Muse but served to ease some friend, not wife,
To help me through this long disease, my life,
To second, Arbuthnot, thy art and care,
And teach the being you preserved to bear.
But why then publish? Granville the polite,          135
And knowing Walsh, would tell me I could write;
Well-natured Garth inflamed with early praise,
And Congreve loved, and Swift endured, my lays;
The courtly Talbot, Somers, Sheffield read,
Even mitred Rochester would nod the head,          140
And St John's self (great Dryden's friends before)
With open arms received one poet more.
Happy my studies, when by these approved!
Happier their author, when by these beloved!
From these the world will judge of men and books,          145
Not from the Burnets, Oldmixons, and Cooks.
Soft were my numbers: who could take offence
While pure description held the place of sense?
Like gentle Fanny's was my flowery theme,
A painted mistress, or a purling stream.          150
Yet then did Gildon draw his venal quill –
I wished the man a dinner, and sate still:
Yet then did Dennis rave in furious fret;
I never answered, I was not in debt:

If want provoked, or madness made them print,                    155
I waged no war with Bedlam or the Mint.
  Did some more sober critic come abroad?
If wrong, I smiled; if right, I kissed the rod.
Pains, reading, study, are their just pretence,
And all they want is spirit, taste, and sense.                    160
Commas and points they set exactly right,
And 'twere a sin to rob them of their mite.
Yet ne'er one sprig of laurel graced these ribalds,
From slashing Bentley down to piddling Tibbalds.
Each wight who reads not, and but scans and spells,                    165
Each word-catcher that lives on syllables,
Even such small critics some regard may claim,
Preserved in Milton's or in Shakespeare's name.
Pretty, in amber to observe the forms
Of hairs, or straws, or dirt, or grubs, or worms!                    170
The things, we know, are neither rich nor rare,
But wonder how the devil they got there!
  Were others angry? I excused them, too;
Well might they rage, I gave them but their due.
A man's true merit 'tis not hard to find,                    175
But each man's secret standard in his mind,
That casting-weight pride adds to emptiness,
This, who can gratify, for who can *guess*?
The bard whom pilfered pastorals renown,
Who turns a Persian tale for half a crown,                    180
Just writes to make his barrenness appear,
And strains, from hard-bound brains, eight lines a year;
He who, still wanting, though he lives on theft;
Steals much, spends little, yet has nothing left;
And he, who now to sense, now nonsense leaning,                    185
Means not, but blunders round about a meaning;
And he whose fustian's so sublimely bad
It is not poetry, but prose run mad:
All these, my modest satire bad translate,
And owned that nine such poets made a Tate.                    190
How did they fume, and stamp, and roar, and chafe,
And swear not Addison himself was safe!
  Peace to all such! But were there one whose fires
True genius kindles and fair fame inspires,

Bless with each talent and each art to please, 195
And born to write, converse, and live with ease:
Should such a man, too fond to rule alone,
Bear, like the Turk, no brother near the throne,
View him with scornful, yet with jealous, eyes,
And hate for arts that caused himself to rise; 200
Damn with faint praise, assent with civil leer,
And without sneering, teach the rest to sneer;
Willing to wound, and yet afraid to strike,
Just hint a fault, and hesitate dislike;
Alike reserved to blame, or to commend, 205
A timorous foe, and a suspicious friend;
Dreading even fools, by flatterers besieged,
And so obliging that he ne'er obliged;
Like Cato, give his little senate laws,
And sit attentive to his own applause; 210
While wits and templars every sentence raise,
And wonder with a foolish face of praise –
Who but must laugh, if such a man there be?
Who would not weep, if Atticus were he!
     What though my name stood rubric on the walls, 215
Or plastered posts, with claps, in capitals?
Or smoking forth, a hundred hawkers' load,
On wings of winds came flying all abroad?
I sought no homage from the race that write;
I kept, like Asian monarchs, from their sight: 220
Poems I heeded (now be-rhymed so long)
No more than thou, great George, a birthday song.
I ne'er with wits or witlings passed my days,
To spread about the itch of verse and praise;
Nor like a puppy daggled through the town, 225
To fetch and carry sing-song up and down;
Nor at rehearsals sweat, and mouthed, and cried,
With handkerchief and orange at my side;
But sick of fops, and poetry, and prate,
To Bufo left the whole Castalian state. 230
     Proud as Apollo on his forked hill
Sat full-blown Bufo, puffed by every quill;
Fed with soft dedication all day long,
Horace and he went hand in hand in song.

His library (where busts of poets dead                         235
And a true Pindar stood without a head)
Received of wits an undistinguished race,
Who first his judgement asked, and then a place.
Much they extolled his pictures, much his seat,
And flattered every day, and some days ate,                    240
Till, grown more frugal in his riper days,
He paid some bards with port, and some with praise.
To some a dry rehearsal was assigned,
And others (harder still) he paid in kind.
Dryden alone (what wonder?) came not nigh,                     245
Dryden alone escaped this judging eye:
But still the great have kindness in reserve –
He helped to bury whom he helped to starve.
   May some choice patron bless each grey goose quill!
May every Bavius have his Bufo still!                          250
So, when a statesman wants a day's defence,
Or envy holds a whole week's war with sense,
Or simple pride for flattery makes demands,
May dunce by dunce be whistled off my hands!
Blessed be the great for those they take away,                 255
And those they left me – for they left me Gay;
Left me to see neglected genius bloom,
Neglected die, and tell it on his tomb;
Of all thy blameless life the sole return
My verse, and Queensbury weeping o'er thy urn!                 260
Oh let me live my own, and die so, too!
('To live and die is all I have to do'):
Maintain a poet's dignity and ease,
And see what friends, and read what books, I please:
Above a patron (though I condescend                            265
Sometimes to call a minister my friend):
I was not born for courts or great affairs;
I pay my debts, believe, and say my prayers;
Can sleep without a poem in my head,
Nor know if Dennis be alive or dead.                           270
   Why am I asked what next shall see the light?
Heavens! Was I born for nothing but to write?
Has life no joys for me? Or (to be grave)
Have I no friend to serve, no soul to save?

'I found him close with Swift' – 'Indeed? No doubt'    275
(Cries prating Balbus) 'something will come out.'
'Tis all in vain, deny it as I will.
'No, such a genius never can lie still';
And then for mine obligingly mistakes
The first lampoon Sir Will or Bubo makes.    280
Poor guiltless I! And can I choose but smile,
When every coxcomb knows me by my style?
    Cursed be the verse, how well soe'er it flow,
That tends to make one worthy man my foe,
Give virtue scandal, innocence a fear,    285
Or from the soft-eyed virgin steal a tear!
But he who hurts a harmless neighbour's peace,
Insults fallen worth, or beauty in distress,
Who loves a lie, lame slander helps about,
Who writes a libel, or who copies out:    290
That fop, whose pride affects a patron's name,
Yet absent, wounds an author's honest fame –
Who can your merit selfishly approve,
And show the sense of it without the love;
Who has the vanity to call you friend,    295
Yet wants the honour, injured, to defend;
Who tells whate'er you think, whate'er you say,
And, if he lie not, must at least betray:
Who to the dean and silver bell can swear,
And sees at Canons what was never there;    300
Who reads but with a lust to misapply,
Make satire a lampoon, and fiction, lie.
A lash like mine no honest man shall dread,
But all such babbling blockheads in his stead.
    Let Sporus tremble – 'What? That thing of silk –    305
Sporus, that mere white curd of ass's milk?
Satire or sense, alas, can Sporus feel?
Who breaks a butterfly upon a wheel?'
Yet let me flap this bug with gilded wings,
This painted child of dirt that stinks and stings;    310
Whose buzz the witty and the fair annoys,
Yet wit ne'er tastes, and beauty ne'er enjoys:
So well-bred spaniels civilly delight
In mumbling of the game they dare not bite.

Eternal smiles his emptiness betray,                                315
As shallow streams run dimpling all the way.
Whether in florid impotence he speaks,
And, as the prompter breathes, the puppet squeaks;
Or at the ear of Eve, familiar toad,
Half froth, half venom, spits himself abroad,                       320
In puns, or politics, or tales, or lies,
Or spite, or smut, or rhymes, or blasphemies.
His wit all see-saw, between that and this,
Now high, now low, now master up, now miss,
And he himself one vile antithesis.                                 325
Amphibious thing that, acting either part –
The trifling head, or the corrupted heart,
Fop at the toilette, flatterer at the board –
Now trips a lady, and now struts a lord.
Eve's tempter thus the rabbins have expressed –                     330
A cherub's face, a reptile all the rest,
Beauty that shocks you, parts that none will trust,
Wit that can creep, and pride that licks the dust.

      Not Fortune's worshipper, nor fashion's fool,
Not lucre's madman, nor ambition's tool,                            335
Not proud, nor servile: be one poet's praise
That, if he pleased, he pleased by manly ways:
That flattery, even to kings, he held a shame,
And thought a lie in verse or prose the same:
That not in fancy's maze he wandered long,                          340
But stooped to truth, and moralised his song:
That not for fame, but virtue's better end,
He stood the furious foe, the timid friend,
The damning critic, half approving wit,
The coxcomb hit, or fearing to be hit;                              345
Laughed at the loss of friends he never had,
The dull, the proud, the wicked, and the mad;
The distant threats of vengeance on his head,
The blow unfelt, the tear he never shed;
The tale revived, the lie so oft o'erthrown;                        350
The imputed trash, and dullness not his own;
The morals blackened when the writings scape,
The libelled person, and the pictured shape;
Abuse, on all he loved, or loved him, spread,

A friend in exile, or a father, dead;                              355
The whisper, that to greatness still too near,
Perhaps yet vibrates on his sovereign's ear –
Welcome for thee, fair Virtue, all the past:
For thee, fair Virtue, welcome even the last.
   'But why insult the poor, affront the great?'                  360
A knave's a knave, to me, in every state:
Alike my scorn, if he succeed or fail,
Sporus at court, or Japhet in a jail,
A hireling scribbler, or a hireling peer,
Knight of the post corrupt, or of the shire;                      365
If on a pillory, or near a throne,
He gain his prince's ear, or lose his own.
   Yet soft by nature, more a dupe than wit,
Sappho can tell you how this man was bit:
This dreaded satirist Dennis will confess                         370
Foe to his pride, but friend to his distress:
So humble, he has knocked at Tibbald's door,
Has drunk with Cibber, nay, has rhymed for Moore.
Full ten years slandered, did he once reply?
Three thousand suns went down on Welsted's lie.                   375
To please a mistress, one aspersed his life;
He lashed him not, but let her be his wife:
Let Budgell charge low Grub Street on his quill,
And write whate'er he pleased, except his will;
Let the two Curlls, of town and court, abuse                      380
His father, mother, body, soul, and Muse.
Yet why? That father held it for a rule
It was a sin to call our neighbour 'fool':
That harmless mother thought no wife a whore:
Hear this, and spare his family, James Moore!                     385
Unspotted names, and memorable long,
If there be force in virtue, or in song.
   Of gentle blood (part shed in honour's cause,
While yet in Britain honour had applause)
Each parent sprung – 'What fortune, pray?' – their own,           390
And better got than Bestia's from the throne.
Born to no pride, inheriting no strife,
Nor marrying discord in a noble wife,
Stranger to civil and religious rage,

The good man walked innoxious through his age.                    395
No courts he saw, no suits would ever try,
Nor dared an oath, nor hazarded a lie:
Unlearned, he knew no schoolman's subtle art,
No language, but the language of the heart.
By nature honest, by experience wise,                    400
Healthy by temperance and by exercise;
His life, though long, to sickness past unknown,
His death was instant, and without a groan.
Oh grant me thus to live, and thus to die,
Who sprung from kings shall know less joy than I.                    405
    Oh friend, may each domestic bliss be thine;
Be no unpleasing melancholy mine:
Me, let the tender office long engage
To rock the cradle of reposing age,
With lenient arts extend a mother's breath,                    410
Make languor smile, and smooth the bed of death,
Explore the thought, explain the asking eye,
And keep a while one parent from the sky!
On cares like these if length of days attend,
May heaven, to bless those days, preserve my friend –                    415
Preserve him social, cheerful, and serene,
And just as rich as when he served a queen!
Whether that blessing be denied or given,
Thus far was right, the rest belongs to heaven.

# Of the Characters of Women:
## An Epistle to a Lady

Nothing so true as what you once let fall,
'Most women have no characters at all.'
Matter too soft a lasting mark to bear,
And best distinguished by black, brown, or fair.
　　How many pictures of one nymph we view – 5
All how unlike each other, all how true!
Arcadia's countess, here, in ermined pride,
Is there, Pastora by a fountain side;
Here Fannia, leering on her own good man,
And there, a naked Leda with a swan. 10
Let then the fair one beautifully cry
In Magdalene's loose hair and lifted eye,
Or dressed in smiles of sweet Cecilia shine,
With simpering angels, palms, and harps divine.
Whether the charmer sinner it, or saint it, 15
If folly grow romantic, I must paint it.
　　Come then, the colours and the ground prepare!
Dip in the rainbow, trick her off in air;
Choose a firm cloud before it fall, and in it
Catch, e'er she change, the Cynthia of this minute. 20
　　Rufa, whose eye, quick-glancing o'er the park,
Attracts each light gay meteor of a spark,
Agrees as ill with Rufa studying Locke,
As Sappho's diamonds with her dirty smock;
Or Sappho at her toilette's greasy task, 25
With Sappho fragrant at an evening masque:
So morning insects, that in muck begun,
Shine, buzz, and fly-blow in the setting sun.
　　How soft is Silia, fearful to offend,
The frail one's advocate, the weak one's friend! 30
To her, Calista proved her conduct nice,
And good Simplicius asks of her advice.
Sudden, she storms, she raves – you tip the wink,
But spare your censure; Silia does not drink.

All eyes may see from what the change arose –                 35
All eyes may see a pimple on her nose.

    Papillia, wedded to her amorous spark,
Sighs for the shades – 'How charming is a park!'
A park is purchased; but the fair he sees
All bathed in tears: 'Oh, odious, odious trees!'              40

    Ladies like variegated tulips show –
'Tis to their changes half their charms we owe;
Their happy spots the nice admirer take,
Fine by defect, and delicately weak.
'Twas thus Calypso once each heart alarmed,                   45
Awed without virtue, without beauty charmed;
Her tongue bewitched as oddly as her eyes,
Less wit than mimic, more a wit than wise;
Strange graces still, and stranger flights she had,
Was just not ugly, and was just not mad;                      50
Yet ne'er so sure our passion to create,
As when she touched the brink of all we hate.

    Narcissa's nature, tolerably mild,
To make a wash would hardly stew a child;
Has even been proved to grant a lover's prayer,              55
And paid a tradesman once to make him stare;
Gave alms at Easter, in a Christian trim,
And made a widow happy, for a whim.
Why then declare good nature is her scorn,
When 'tis by that alone she can be born?                      60
Why pique all mortals, yet affect a name –
A fool to pleasure, yet a slave to fame:
Now deep in Taylor and the *Book of Martyrs*,
Now drinking citron with his grace and Chartres:
Now conscience chills her, and now passion burns;           65
And atheism and religion take their turns;
A very heathen in the carnal part,
Yet still a sad, good Christian at her heart.

    See sin in state, majestically drunk,
Proud as a peeress, prouder as a punk;                       70
Chaste to her husband, frank to all beside,
A teeming mistress, but a barren bride.
What then? Let blood and body bear the fault,
Her head's untouched (that noble seat of thought):

Such this day's doctrine – in another fit                        75
She sins with poets through pure love of wit.
What has not fired her bosom or her brain?
Cæsar and Tallboy, Charles and Charlemagne.
As Helluo, late dictator of the feast,
The nose of haut-gout, and the tip of taste,             80
Critic-ed your wine and analysed your meat,
Yet on plain pudding deigned at home to eat;
So Philomede, lecturing all mankind
On the soft passion and the taste refined,
The address, the delicacy – stoops at once,              85
And makes her hearty meal upon a dunce.
    Flavia's a wit, has too much sense to pray;
To toast our wants and wishes is her way;
Nor asks of God, but of her stars, to give
The mighty blessing, 'while we live, to live.'            90
Then all for death, that opiate of the soul –
Lucretia's dagger, Rosamonda's bowl.
Say, what can cause such impotence of mind? –
A spark too fickle, or a spouse too kind.
Wise wretch, with pleasures too refined to please,       95
With too much spirit to be e'er at ease,
With too much quickness ever to be taught,
With too much thinking to have common thought:
You purchase pain with all that joy can give,
And die of nothing but a rage to live.                   100
    Turn then from wits, and look on Simo's mate –
No ass so meek, no ass so obstinate;
Or her, that owns her faults, but never mends,
Because she's honest, and the best of friends;
Or her, whose life the church and scandal share,        105
For ever in a passion, or a prayer;
Or her, who laughs at hell, but (like her grace)
Cries, 'Ah! how charming if there's no such place!'
Or who in sweet vicissitude appears
Of mirth and opium, ratafie and tears –                  110
The daily anodyne and nightly draught,
To kill those foes to fair ones, time and thought.
Woman and fool are two hard things to hit;
For true no-meaning puzzles more than wit.

But what are these to great Atossa's mind?                          115
Scarce once herself, by turns all womankind!
Who, with herself, or others, from her birth
Finds all her life one warfare upon earth:
Shines in exposing knaves, and painting fools,
Yet is whate'er she hates and ridicules.                            120
No thought advances, but her eddy brain
Whisks it about, and down it goes again.
Full sixty years the world has been her trade,
The wisest fool much time has ever made.
From loveless youth to unrespected age,                             125
No passion gratified except her rage.
So much the fury still outran the wit,
The pleasure missed her, and the scandal hit.
Who breaks with her, provokes revenge from hell,
But he's a bolder man who dares be well.                            130
Her every turn with violence pursued,
Nor more a storm her hate than gratitude:
To that each passion turns, or soon or late;
Love, if it makes her yield, must make her hate.
Superiors? Death! And equals? What a curse!                         135
But an inferior not dependent? worse.
Offend her, and she knows not to forgive;
Oblige her, and she'll hate you while you live.
But die, and she'll adore you – then the bust
And temple rise – then fall again to dust.                          140
Last night, her lord was all that's good and great;
A knave this morning, and his will a cheat.
Strange! By the means defeated of the ends,
By spirit robbed of power, by warmth of friends,
By wealth of followers! Without one distress                        145
Sick of herself through very selfishness!
Atossa, cursed with every granted prayer,
Childless with all her children, wants an heir.
To heirs unknown descends the unguarded store
Or wanders, heaven-directed, to the poor.                           150
    Pictures like these, dear madam, to design,
Asks no firm hand, and no unerring line;
Some wandering touches, some reflected light,
Some flying stroke alone can hit 'em right:

For how should equal colours do the knack? 155
Chameleons who can paint in white and black?
    'Yet Chloe sure was formed without a spot' –
Nature in her then erred not, but forgot.
'With every pleasing, every prudent part,
Say, what can Chloe want?' – she wants a heart. 160
She speaks, behaves, and acts just as she ought;
But never, never, reached one generous thought.
Virtue she finds too painful an endeavour,
Content to dwell in decencies for ever.
So very reasonable, so unmoved, 165
As never yet to love, or to be loved.
She, while her lover pants upon her breast,
Can mark the figures on an Indian chest;
And when she sees her friend in deep despair,
Observes how much a chintz exceeds mohair. 170
Forbid it, heaven, a favour or a debt
She e'er should cancel – but she may forget.
Safe is your secret still in Chloe's ear;
But none of Chloe's shall you ever hear.
Of all her dears she never slandered one, 175
But cares not if a thousand are undone.
Would Chloe know if you're alive or dead?
She bids her footman put it in her head.
Chloe is prudent – would you, too, be wise?
Then never break your heart when Chloe dies. 180
    One certain portrait may (I grant) be seen,
Which heaven has varnished out, and made a queen:
The same for ever, and described by all
With truth and goodness, as with crown and ball.
Poets heap virtues, painters gems at will, 185
And show their zeal, and hide their want of skill –
'Tis well; but, artists who can paint or write,
To draw the naked is your true delight.
That robe of quality so struts and swells,
None see what parts or nature it conceals: 190
The exactest traits of body or of mind
We owe to models of an humble kind.
If Queensberry to strip there's no compelling,
'Tis from a handmaid we must take a Helen.

From peer or bishop 'tis no easy thing                    195
To draw the man who loves his God or king:
Alas! I copy (or my draught would fail)
From honest Mahomet, or plain Parson Hale.

    But grant, in public men sometimes are shown,
A woman's seen in private life alone:                    200
Our bolder talents in full light displayed;
Your virtues open fairest in the shade.
Bred to disguise, in public 'tis you hide;
There, none distinguish 'twixt your shame or pride,
Weakness or delicacy – all so nice,                    205
That each may seem a virtue, or a vice.

    In men, we various ruling passions find;
In women, two almost divide the kind;
Those, only fixed, they first or last obey,
The love of pleasure, and the love of sway.                    210

    That, nature gives; and where the lesson taught
Is but to please, can pleasure seem a fault?
Experience, this; by man's oppression cursed
They seek the second not to lose the first.

    Men, some to business, some to pleasure take;                    215
But every woman is at heart a rake:
Men, some to quiet, some to public strife;
But every lady would be queen for life.

    Yet mark the fate of a whole sex of queens!
Power all their end, but beauty all the means:                    220
In youth they conquer with so wild a rage,
As leaves them scarce a subject in their age:
For foreign glory, foreign joy, they roam;
No thought of peace or happiness at home.
But wisdom's triumph is well-timed retreat,                    225
As hard a science to the fair as great!
Beauties, like tyrants, old and friendless grown,
Yet hate repose, and dread to be alone,
Worn out in public, weary every eye,
Nor leave one sigh behind them when they die.                    230

    Pleasures the sex, as children birds, pursue,
Still out of reach, yet never out of view;
Sure, if they catch, to spoil the toy at most,
To covet flying, and regret when lost:

At last, to follies youth could scarce defend,                    235
It grows their age's prudence to pretend;
Ashamed to own they gave delight before,
Reduced to feign it, when they give no more:
As hags hold sabbaths less for joy than spite,
So these their merry, miserable night.                    240
Still round and round the ghosts of beauty glide,
And haunt the places where their honour died.
    See how the world its veterans rewards!
A youth of frolics, an old age of cards;
Fair to no purpose, artful to no end,                    245
Young without lovers, old without a friend;
A fop their passion, but their prize a sot,
Alive, ridiculous, and dead, forgot!
    Ah, friend, to dazzle let the vain design;
To raise the thought, and touch the heart, be thine!                    250
That charm shall grow, while what fatigues the Ring,
Flaunts and goes down, an unregarded thing:
So, when the sun's broad beam has tired the sight,
All mild ascends the moon's more sober light,
Serene in virgin modesty she shines,                    255
And unobserved the glaring orb declines.
    Oh! blessed with temper, whose unclouded ray
Can make tomorrow cheerful as today!
She, who can love a sister's charms, or hear
Sighs for a daughter with unwounded ear;                    260
She, who ne'er answers till a husband cools,
Or, if she rules him, never shows she rules;
Charms by accepting, by submitting sways,
Yet has her humour most when she obeys;
Lets fops or Fortune fly which way they will;                    265
Disdains all loss of tickets, or codille;
Spleen, vapours, or smallpox, above them all,
And mistress of herself, though china fall.
    And yet, believe me, good as well as ill,
Woman's at best a contradiction still.                    270
Heaven, when it strives to polish all it can
Its last best work, but forms a softer man;
Picks from each sex, to make the favourite blessed,
Your love of pleasure, our desire of rest:

Blends, in exception to all general rules,                                   275
Your taste of follies with our scorn of fools,
Reserve with frankness, art with truth allied,
Courage with softness, modesty with pride,
Fixed principles, with fancy ever new;
Shakes all together, and produces – you.                                     280
    Be this a woman's fame: with this unblessed,
Toasts live a scorn, and queens may die a jest.
This Phœbus promised (I forget the year)
When those blue eyes first opened on the sphere;
Ascendant Phœbus watched that hour with care,                                285
Averted half your parents' simple prayer,
And gave you beauty, but denied the pelf
That buys your sex a tyrant o'er itself.
The generous god, who wit and gold refines,
And ripens spirits as he ripens mines,                                       290
Kept dross for duchesses, the world shall know it,
To you gave sense, good-humour, and a poet.

# The Dunciad,

## in Four Books

### BOOK 1

The mighty mother, and her son who brings
The Smithfield Muses to the ear of kings,
I sing. Say you, her instruments, the great,
Called to this work by Dullness, Jove, and Fate;
You by whose care, in vain decried and cursed,                 5
Still Dunce the second reigns like Dunce the first;
Say how the goddess bade Britannia sleep,
And poured her spirit o'er the land and deep.

   In eldest time, e'er mortals writ or read,
E'er Pallas issued from the Thunderer's head,                 10
Dullness o'er all possessed her ancient right,
Daughter of Chaos and eternal Night:
Fate in their dotage this fair idiot gave,
Gross as her sire, and as her mother grave,
Laborious, heavy, busy, bold, and blind,                      15
She ruled, in native anarchy, the mind.

   Still her old empire to restore she tries,
For, born a goddess, Dullness never dies.

   Oh thou! whatever title please thine ear,
Dean, Drapier, Bickerstaff, or Gulliver!                      20
Whether thou choose Cervantes' serious air,
Or laugh and shake in Rabelais' easy chair,
Or praise the court, or magnify mankind,
Or thy grieved country's copper chains unbind;
From thy Bœotia though her power retires,                     25
Mourn not, my Swift, at aught our realm acquires,
Here pleased behold her mighty wings outspread
To hatch a new Saturnian age of lead.

   Close to those walls where Folly holds her throne,
And laughs to think Monroe would take her down,               30
Where o'er the gates, by his famed father's hand,
Great Cibber's brazen, brainless brothers stand,

One cell there is, concealed from vulgar eye,
The cave of Poverty and Poetry:
Keen, hollow winds howl through the bleak recess,          35
Emblem of music caused by emptiness.
Hence bards, like Proteus long in vain tied down,
Escape in monsters, and amaze the town.
Hence miscellanies spring, the weekly boast
Of Curll's chaste press, and Lintot's rubric post:          40
Hence hymning Tyburn's elegiac lines,
Hence journals, medleys, Mercuries, magazines:
Sepulchral lies, our holy walls to grace,
And new-year odes, and all the Grub Street race.

In clouded majesty here Dullness shone;                    45
Four guardian virtues, round, support her throne:
Fierce champion Fortitude, that knows no fears
Of hisses, blows, or want, or loss of ears;
Calm Temperance, whose blessings those partake
Who hunger, and who thirst for scribbling's sake;          50
Prudence, whose glass presents the approaching jail:
Poetic Justice, with her lifted scale,
Where, in nice balance, truth with gold she weighs,
And solid pudding against empty praise.

Here she beholds the chaos dark and deep                   55
Where nameless somethings in their causes sleep,
'Till genial Jacob, or a warm third day,
Call forth each mass, a poem, or a play:
How hints, like spawn, scarce quick in embryo lie,
How new-born nonsense first is taught to cry,              60
Maggots half-formed in rhyme exactly meet,
And learn to crawl upon poetic feet.
Here one poor word an hundred clenches makes,
And ductile dullness new meanders takes;
There motley images her fancy strike,                      65
Figures ill-paired, and similes unlike.
She sees a mob of metaphors advance,
Pleased with the madness of the mazy dance:
How tragedy and comedy embrace;
How farce and epic get a jumbled race;                     70
How Time himself stands still at her command,
Realms shift their place, and ocean turns to land.

Here gay description Egypt glads with showers,
Or gives to Zembla fruits, to Barca flowers;
Glittering with ice here hoary hills are seen,                    75
There painted valleys of eternal green;
In cold December fragrant chaplets blow,
And heavy harvests nod beneath the snow.
      All these, and more, the cloud-compelling queen
Beholds through fogs, that magnify the scene.                     80
She, tinselled o'er in robes of varying hues,
With self-applause her wild creation views –
Sees momentary monsters rise and fall,
And with her own fools-colours gilds them all.
      'Twas on the day when * * rich and grave,                   85
Like Cimon, triumphed both on land and wave
(Pomps without guilt, of bloodless swords and maces,
Glad chains, warm furs, broad banners, and broad faces).
Now night descending, the proud scene was o'er,
But lived, in Settle's numbers, one day more.                     90
Now mayors and shrieves all hushed and satiate lay,
Yet ate, in dreams, the custard of the day;
While pensive poets painful vigils keep,
Sleepless themselves to give their readers sleep.
Much to the mindful queen the feast recalls                       95
What city swans once sung within the walls;
Much she revolves their arts, their ancient praise,
And sure succession down from Heywood's days.
She saw, with joy, the line immortal run,
Each sire impressed and glaring in his son:                      100
So watchful bruin forms, with plastic care,
Each growing lump, and brings it to a bear.
She saw old Prynne in restless Daniel shine,
And Eusden eke out Blackmore's endless line;
She saw slow Philips creep like Tate's poor page,                105
And all the mighty mad in Dennis rage.
      In each she marks her image full expressed,
But chief in Bays's monster-breeding breast;
Bays, formed by nature stage and town to bless,
And act, and be, a coxcomb with success.                         110
Dullness with transport eyes the lively dunce,
Remembering she herself was pertness once.

Now (shame to Fortune!) an ill run at play
Blanked his bold visage, and a thin third day:
Swearing and supperless the hero sat,                         115
Blasphemed his gods, the dice, and damned his fate;
Then gnawed his pen, then dashed it on the ground,
Sinking from thought to thought, a vast profound!
Plunged for his sense, but found no bottom there,
Yet wrote and floundered on, in mere despair.                 120
Round him much embryo, much abortion lay,
Much future ode, and abdicated play;
Nonsense precipitate, like running lead,
That slipped through cracks and zig-zags of the head;
All that on folly frenzy could bget,                          125
Fruits of dull heat, and sooterkins of wit.
Next, o'er his books his eyes began to roll,
In pleasing memory of all he stole,
How here he sipped, how there he plundered snug
And sucked all o'er, like an industrious bug.                 130
Here lay poor Fletcher's half-ate scenes, and here
The frippery of crucified Molière;
There hapless Shakespeare, yet of Tibbald sore,
Wished he had blotted for himself before.
The rest on outside merit but presume,                        135
Or serve (like other fools) to fill a room;
Such with their shelves as due proportion hold,
Or their fond parents dressed in red and gold;
Or where the pictures for the page atone,
And Quarles is saved by beauties not his own.                 140
Here swells the shelf with Ogilby the great;
There, stamped with arms, Newcastle shines complete:
Here all his suffering brotherhood retire,
And 'scape the martyrdom of jakes and fire:
A gothic library, of Greece and Rome                          145
Well purged, and worthy Settle, Banks, and Broome.
    But, high above, more solid learning shone,
The classics of an age that heard of none;
There Caxton slept, with Wynkyn at his side,
One clasped in wood, and one in strong cow-hide;              150
There, saved by spice, like mummies, many a year,
Dry bodies of divinity appear:

De Lyra there a dreadful front extends,
And here the groaning shelves Philemon bends.
   Of these twelve volumes, twelve of amplest size, 155
Redeemed from tapers and defrauded pies,
Inspired he seizes: these an altar raise:
An hecatomb of pure, unsullied lays
That altar crowns: a folio common-place
Founds the whole pile, of all his works the base: 160
Quartos, octavos, shape the lessening pyre;
A twisted birthday ode completes the spire.
   Then he: 'Great tamer of all human art!
First in my care, and ever at my heart;
Dullness! Whose good old cause I yet defend, 165
With whom my Muse began, with whom shall end;
E'er since Sir Fopling's periwig was praise,
To the last honours of the butt and bays:
Oh thou, of business the directing soul!
To this our head like bias to the bowl, 170
Which, as more ponderous, made its aim more true,
Obliquely waddling to the mark in view:
Oh ever gracious to perplexed mankind,
Still spread a healing mist before the mind;
And, lest we err by wit's wild dancing light, 175
Secure us kindly in our native night.
Or, if to wit a coxcomb make pretence,
Guard the sure barrier between that and sense;
Or quite unravel all the reasoning thread,
And hang some curious cobweb in its stead! 180
As, forced from wind-guns, lead itself can fly,
And ponderous slugs cut swiftly through the sky;
As clocks to weight their nimble motion owe,
The wheels above urged by the load below:
Me emptiness, and Dullness could inspire, 185
And were my elasticity, and fire.
Some demon stole my pen (forgive the offence)
And once betrayed me into common sense:
Else all my prose and verse were much the same –
This, prose on stilts, that, poetry fallen lame. 190
Did on the stage my fops appear confined?
My life gave ampler lessons to mankind.

Did the dead letter unsuccessful prove?
The brisk example never failed to move.
Yet sure had heaven decreed to save the state, 195
Heaven had decreed these works a longer date.
Could Troy be saved by any single hand,
This grey-goose weapon must have made her stand.
What can I now? My Fletcher cast aside,
Take up the Bible, once my better guide? 200
Or tread the path by venturous heroes trod,
This box my thunder, this right hand my god?
Or chaired at White's amidst the doctors sit,
Teach oaths to gamesters, and to nobles wit?
Or bidst thou rather party to embrace? 205
(A friend to Party thou, and all her race;
'Tis the same rope at different ends they twist;
To Dullness Ridpath is as dear as Mist.)
Shall I, like Curtius, desperate in my zeal,
O'er head and ears plunge for the commonweal? 210
Or rob Rome's ancient geese of all their glories,
And cackling save the monarchy of Tories?
Hold – to the minister I more incline –
To serve his cause, oh queen, is serving thine!
And see! Thy very gazetteers give o'er, 215
Ev'n Ralph repents, and Henley writes no more.
What then remains? Ourself. Still, still remain
Cibberian forehead, and Cibberian brain.
This brazen brightness, to the squire so dear;
This polished hardness, that reflects the peer; 220
This arch absurd, that wit and fool delights;
This mess, tossed up of Hockley Hole and White's;
Where dukes and butchers join to wreathe my crown,
At once the bear and fiddle of the town.
  Oh born in sin, and forth in folly brought, 225
Works damned, or to be damned (your father's fault) –
Go, purified by flames ascend the sky,
My better and more Christian progeny!
Unstained, untouched, and yet in maiden sheets.
While all your smutty sisters walk the streets. 230
Ye shall not beg, like gratis-given Bland,
Sent with a pass, and vagrant through the land;

Not sail, with Ward, to ape-and-monkey climes,
Where vile mundungus trucks for viler rhymes;
Not sulphur-tipped, emblaze an alehouse fire;                235
Not wrap up oranges, to pelt your sire!
Oh, pass more innocent, in infant state,
To the mild limbo of our father, Tate:
Or, peaceably forgot, at once be blessed
In Shadwell's bosom with eternal rest!                       240
Soon to that mass of nonsense to return,
Where things destroyed are swept to things unborn.'
    With that, a tear (portentous sign of grace!)
Stole from the master of the sevenfold face:
And thrice he lifted high the birthday brand,               245
And thrice he dropped it from his quivering hand;
Then lights the structure, with averted eyes:
The rolling smokes involve the sacrifice.
The opening clouds disclose each work by turns,
Now flames the Cid, and now Perolla burns;                   250
Great Cæsar roars, and hisses in the fires;
King John in silence modestly expires:
No merit now the dear nonjuror claims,
Molière's old stubble in a moment flames.
Tears gushed again, as from pale Priam's eyes               255
When the last blaze sent Ilion to the skies.
    Roused by the light, old Dullness heaved the head,
Then snatched a sheet of Thulè from her bed;
Sudden she flies, and whelms it o'er the pyre;
Down sink the flames, and with a hiss expire.               260
    Her ample presence fills up all the place;
A veil of fogs dilates her awful face:
Great in her charms, as when on shrieves and mayors
She looks, and breathes herself into their airs.
She bids him wait her to her sacred dome:                    265
Well pleased he entered, and confessed his home.
So spirits, ending their terrestrial race,
Ascend, and recognise their native place.
This the great mother dearer held than all
The clubs of quidnuncs, or her own Guildhall:               270
Here stood her opium, here she nursed her owls,
And here she planned the imperial seat of fools.

Here to her chosen all her works she shows;
Prose swelled to verse, verse loitering into prose:
How random thoughts now meaning chance to find,                    275
Now leave all memory of sense behind:
How prologues into prefaces decay,
And these to notes are frittered quite away;
How index-learning turns no student pale,
Yet holds the eel of science by the tail;                          280
How, with less reading than makes felons 'scape,
Less human genius than God gives an ape,
Small thanks to France, and none to Rome or Greece,
A past, vamped, future, old, revived, new piece,
'Twixt Plautus, Fletcher, Shakespeare, and Corneille,             285
Can make a Cibber, Tibbald, or Ozell.
    The goddess then, o'er his anointed head,
With mystic words the sacred opium shed.
And lo! her bird (a monster of a fowl,
Something betwixt a Heidegger and owl)                            290
Perched on his crown: 'All hail! And hail again,
My son! The promised land expects thy reign.
Know, Eusden thirsts no more for sack or praise:
He sleeps among the dull of ancient days;
Safe, where no critics damn, no duns molest,                      295
Where wretched Withers, Ward, and Gildon rest,
And high-born Howard, more majestic sire,
With fool of quality completes the choir.
Thou, Cibber, thou, his laurel shalt support,
Folly, my son, has still a friend at court.                       300
Lift up your gates, ye princes, see him come!
Sound, sound ye viols, be the cat-call dumb!
Bring, bring the madding bay, the drunken vine;
The creeping, dirty, courtly ivy join.
And thou, his aide de camp, lead on my sons,                      305
Light-armed with points, antitheses, and puns.
Let Bawdry, Billingsgate, my daughters dear,
Support his front, and oaths bring up the rear:
And under his, and under Archer's wing,
Gaming and Grub Street skulk behind the king.                     310
    Oh, when shall rise a monarch all our own,
And I, a nursing-mother, rock the throne,

'Twixt prince and people close the curtain draw,
Shade him from light, and cover him from law;
Fatten the courtier, starve the learned band,                          315
And suckle armies, and dry-nurse the land:
'Till senates nod to lullabies divine,
And all be sleep, as at an ode of thine.'

    She ceased. Then swells the Chapel-royal throat:
'God save king Cibber!' mounts in every note.                          320
Familiar White's, 'God save king Colley!' cries;
'God save king Colley!' Drury Lane replies.
To Needham's quick the voice triumphal rode,
But pious Needham dropped the name of God;
Back to the devil the last echoes roll,                                325
And 'Coll!' each butcher roars at Hockley Hole.
    So when Jove's block descended from on high
(As sings thy great forefather Ogilby)
Loud thunder to its bottom shook the bog,
And the hoarse nation croaked, 'God save king Log!'                    330

## BOOK 4

Yet, yet a moment, one dim ray of light
Indulge, dread Chaos, and eternal Night!
Of darkness visible so much be lent,
As half to show, half veil the deep intent.
Ye powers, whose mysteries restored I sing,                            5
To whom Time bears me on his rapid wing,
Suspend a while your force inertly strong,
Then take at once the poet and the song.
    Now flamed the dog-star's unpropitious ray,
Smote every brain, and withered every bay;                             10
Sick was the sun, the owl forsook his bower,
The moon-struck prophet felt the madding hour:
Then rose the seed of Chaos and of Night,
To blot out order, and extinguish light,
Of dull and venal a new world to mould,                                15
And bring Saturnian days of lead and gold.
    She mounts the throne: her head a cloud concealed,
In broad effulgence all below revealed

('Tis thus aspiring Dullness ever shines);
Soft on her lap her laureate son reclines.                    20
    Beneath her foot-stool, Science groans in chains,
And Wit dreads exile, penalties and pains.
There foamed rebellious Logic, gagged and bound,
There, stripped, fair Rhetoric languished on the ground;
His blunted arms by Sophistry are born,                      25
And shameless Billingsgate her robes adorn.
Morality, by her false guardians drawn,
Chicane in Furs, and Casuistry in lawn,
Gasps, as they straiten at each end the cord,
And dies, when Dullness gives her page the word.            30
Mad Mathesis alone was unconfined,
Too mad for mere material chains to bind,
Now to pure space lifts her ecstatic stare,
Now running round the circle, finds it square.
But held in tenfold bonds the Muses lie,                     35
Watched both by Envy's and by Flattery's eye:
There to her heart sad Tragedy addressed
The dagger wont to pierce the tyrant's breast;
But sober History restrained her rage,
And promised vengeance on a barbarous age.                  40
There sunk Thalia, nerveless, cold, and dead,
Had not her sister satyr held her head:
Nor couldest thou, Chesterfield, a tear refuse:
Thou weptest, and with thee wept each gentle Muse.
    When lo! A harlot form soft sliding by,                  45
With mincing step, small voice, and languid eye;
Foreign her air, her robe's discordant pride
In patchwork fluttering, and her head aside:
By singing peers upheld on either hand,
She tripped and laughed, too pretty much to stand;          50
Cast on the prostrate nine a scornful look,
Then thus in quaint recitativo spoke.
'Oh *Cara! Cara!* Silence all that train:
Joy to great Chaos! Let Division reign:
Chromatic tortures soon shall drive them hence,             55
Break all their nerves, and fritter all their sense:
One trill shall harmonise joy, grief, and rage,
Wake the dull Church, and lull the ranting stage;

To the same notes thy sons shall hum, or snore,
And all thy yawning daughters cry, *encore*.                    60
Another Phœbus, thy own Phœbus, reigns,
Joys in my jigs, and dances in my chains.
But soon, ah soon, rebellion will commence,
If music meanly borrows aid from sense:
Strong in new arms, lo! giant Handel stands,                    65
Like bold Briareus, with a hundred hands;
To stir, to rouse, to shake the soul he comes,
And Jove's own thunders follow Mars's drums.
Arrest him, empress, or you sleep no more.'
She heard, and drove him to the Hibernian shore.                70
    And now had Fame's posterior trumpet blown,
And all the nations summoned to the throne.
The young, the old, who feel her inward sway,
One instinct seizes, and transports away.
None need a guide, by sure attraction led,                      75
And strong impulsive gravity of head:
None want a place, for all their centre found,
Hung to the goddess, and cohered around.
Not closer, orb in orb, conglobed are seen
The buzzing bees about their dusky queen.                       80
    The gathering number, as it moves along,
Involves a vast involuntary throng,
Who gently drawn, and struggling less and less,
Roll in her vortex, and her power confess.
Not those alone who passive own her laws,                       85
But who, weak rebels, more advance her cause.
Whate'er of dunce in college or in town
Sneers at another, in toupée or gown;
Whatever of mongrel no one class admits,
A wit with dunces, and a dunce with wits.                       90
    Nor absent they, no members of her state,
Who pay her homage in her sons, the great
Who, false to Phœbus, bow the knee to Baal,
Or, impious, preach his word without a call.
Patrons, who sneak from living worth to dead,                   95
Withhold the pension, and set up the head;
Or vest dull Flattery in the sacred gown;
Or give from fool to fool the laurel crown.

And (last and worst) with all the cant of wit,
Without the soul, the Muse's hypocrite.                         100
  There marched the bard and blockhead, side by side,
Who rhymed for hire, and patronised for pride.
Narcissus, praised with all a parson's power,
Looked a white lily sunk beneath a shower.
There moved Montalto with superior air,                         105
His stretched-out arm displayed a volume fair.
Courtiers and Patriots in two ranks divide –
Through both he passed, and bowed from side to side;
But as in graceful act, with awful eye
Composed he stood, bold Benson thrust him by:                   110
On two unequal crutches propped he came,
Milton's on this, on that one Johnston's name.
The decent knight retired with sober rage,
Withdrew his hand, and closed the pompous page.

   *       *       *       *       *       *       *
   *       *       *       *       *       *       *
   *       *       *       *       *       *       *
   *       *       *       *       *       *       *

  When Dullness, smiling: 'Thus revive the wits!
But murder first, and mince them all to bits;                   120
As erst Medea (cruel, so to save!)
A new edition of old Æson gave,
Let standard authors thus, like trophies born,
Appear more glorious as more hacked and torn,
And you, my critics, in the chequered shade,                    125
Admire new light through holes yourselves have made.
  Leave not a foot of verse, a foot of stone,
A page, a grave, that they can call their own;
But spread, my sons, your glory thin or thick,
On passive paper, or on solid brick.                            130
So by each bard an alderman shall sit,
A heavy lord shall hang at every wit,
And while on Fame's triumphal car they ride,
Some slave of mine be pinioned to their side.'
  Now crowds on crowds around the goddess press,                135
Each eager to present the first address.
Dunce scorning dunce beholds the next advance,
But fop shows fop superior complaisance.

When lo! A spectre rose, whose index hand
Held forth the virtue of the dreadful wand;                    140
His beavered brow a birchen garland wears,
Dropping with infant's blood, and mother's tears.
O'er every vein a shuddering horror runs;
Eton and Winton shake through all their sons.
All flesh is humbled, Westminster's bold race                  145
Shrink, and confess the genius of the place:
The pale boy-senator yet tingling stands,
And holds his breeches close with both his hands.
   Then thus. 'Since man from beast by words is known,
Words are man's province, words we teach alone.               150
When Reason doubtful, like the Samian letter,
Points him two ways, the narrower is the better.
Placed at the door of learning, youth to guide,
We never suffer it to stand too wide.
To ask, to guess, to know, as they commence,                  155
As fancy opens the quick springs of sense,
We ply the memory, we load the brain,
Bind rebel wit, and double chain on chain,
Confine the thought, to exercise the breath,
And keep them in the pale of words till death.                160
Whate'er the talents, or howe'er designed,
We hang one jingling padlock on the mind:
A poet the first day, he dips his quill;
And what the last? A very poet still.
Pity! The charm works only in our wall,                       165
Lost, lost too soon in yonder House or Hall.
There truant Wyndham every Muse gave o'er,
There Talbot sunk, and was a wit no more!
How sweet an Ovid, Murray was our boast!
How many Martials were in Pulteney lost!                      170
Else sure some bard, to our eternal praise,
In twice ten thousand rhyming nights and days,
Had reached the work, the all that mortal can;
And South beheld that masterpiece of man.'
   'Oh' (cried the goddess) 'for some pedant reign!            175
Some gentle James, to bless the land again;
To stick the doctor's chair into the throne,
Give law to words, or war with words alone,

Senates and courts with Greek and Latin rule,
And turn the council to a grammar school!                    180
For sure, if Dullness sees a grateful day,
'Tis in the shade of arbitrary sway.
Oh, if my sons may learn one earthly thing,
Teach but that one, sufficient for a king;
That which my priests, and mine alone, maintain,            185
Which as it dies, or lives, we fall, or reign:
May you, may Cam, and Isis preach it long!
"The Right Divine of kings to govern wrong." '
    Prompt at the call, around the goddess roll
Broad hats, and hoods, and caps, a sable shoal:            190
Thick, and more thick, the black blockade extends,
A hundred head of Aristotle's friends.
Nor wert thou, Isis, wanting to the day
[Tho' Christ Church long kept prudishly away.]
Each staunch polemic, stubborn as a rock,                  195
Each fierce logician, still expelling Locke,
Came whip and spur, and dashed through thin and thick
On German Crousaz, and Dutch Burgersdyck.
As many quit the streams that murmuring fall
To lull the sons of Margaret and Clare Hall,               200
Where Bentley late tempestuous wont to sport
In troubled waters, but now sleeps in port.
Before them marched that awful Aristarch;
Ploughed was his front with many a deep remark:
His hat, which never vailed to human pride,                205
Walker with reverence took, and laid aside.
Low bowed the rest: he, kingly, did but nod;
So upright quakers please both man and God:
'Mistress! Dismiss that rabble from your throne:
Avaunt – is Aristarchus yet unknown?                       210
Thy mighty scholiast, whose unwearied pains
Made Horace dull, and humbled Milton's strains.
Turn what they will to verse, their toil is vain,
Critics like me shall make it prose again.
Roman and Greek grammarians, know your better:            215
Author of something yet more great than letter;
While towering o'er your alphabet, like Saul,
Stands our digamma, and o'ertops them all.

'Tis true, on words is still our whole debate,
Disputes of *Me* or *Te* of *aut* or *at*,                    220
To sound or sink in *cano*, O or A,
Or give up Cicero to C or K.
Let Friend affect to speak as Terence spoke,
And Alsop never but like Horace joke:
For me, what Virgil, Pliny may deny,                          225
Manilius or Solinus shall supply:
For Attic phrase in Plato let them seek,
I poach in Suidas for unlicensed Greek.
In ancient sense if any needs will deal,
Be sure I give them fragments, not a meal;                    230
What Gellius or Stobæus hashed before,
Or chewed by blind old scholiasts o'er and o'er.
The critic eye, that microscope of wit,
Sees hairs and pores, examines bit by bit:
How parts relate to parts, or they to whole,                  235
The body's harmony, the beaming soul,
Are things which Kuster, Burmann, Wasse shall see,
When man's whole frame is obvious to a flea.
    Ah, think not, mistress, more true dullness lies
In folly's cap than wisdom's grave disguise.                  240
Like buoys, that never sink into the flood,
On learning's surface we but lie and nod.
Thine is the genuine head of many a house,
And much divinity without a *nous*.
Nor could a Barrow work on every block,                       245
Nor has one Atterbury spoiled the flock.
See! still thy own, the heavy cannon roll,
And metaphysic smokes involve the pole.
For thee we dim the eyes, and stuff the head
With all such reading as was never read:                      250
For thee explain a thing till all men doubt it,
And write about it, goddess, and about it:
So spins the silkworm small its slender store,
And labours till it clouds itself all o'er.
    What though we let some better sort of fool               255
Thread every science, run through every school?
Never by tumbler through the hoops was shown
Such skill in passing all, and touching none.

He may, indeed (if sober all this time),
Plague with dispute, or persecute with rhyme.                    260
We only furnish what he cannot use,
Or wed to what he must divorce, a Muse.
Full in the midst of Euclid dip at once,
And petrify a genius to a dunce:
Or set on metaphysic ground to prance,                           265
Show all his paces, not a step advance.
With the same cement, ever sure to bind,
We bring to one dead level every mind.
Then take him to develop, if you can,
And hew the block off, and get out the man.                      270
But wherefore waste I words? I see advance
Whore, pupil, and laced governor from France.
Walker! our hat' – nor more he deigned to say,
But, stern as Ajax' spectre, strode away,
   In flowed at once a gay embroidered race,                     275
And tittering pushed the pedants off the place:
Some would have spoken, but the voice was drowned
By the French horn, or by the opening hound.
The first came forwards, with as easy mien,
As if he saw St James's and the queen.                           280
When thus the attendant orator begun:
'Receive, great empress, thy accomplished son:
Thine from the birth, and sacred from the rod,
A dauntless infant, never scared with God.
The sire saw, one by one, his virtues wake:                      285
The mother begged the blessing of a rake.
Thou gavest that ripeness, which so soon began,
And ceased so soon, he ne'er was boy, nor man.
Through school and college, thy kind cloud o'ercast,
Safe and unseen the young Æneas passed:                          290
Thence bursting glorious, all at once let down,
Stunned with his giddy 'larum half the town.
Intrepid then, o'er seas and lands he flew:
Europe he saw, and Europe saw him, too.
There all thy gifts and graces we display,                       295
Thou, only thou, directing all our way!
To where the Seine, obsequious as she runs,
Pours at great Bourbon's feet her silken sons;

Or Tiber, now no longer Roman, rolls,
Vain of Italian arts, Italian souls,                              300
To happy convents, bosomed deep in vines;
Where slumber abbots, purple as their wines;
To isles of fragrance, lily-silvered vales,
Diffusing languor in the panting gales:
To lands of singing, or of dancing slaves,                        305
Love-whispering woods, and lute-resounding waves.
But chief her shrine where naked Venus keeps,
And Cupids ride the lion of the deeps;
Where, eased of fleets, the Adriatic main
Wafts the smooth eunuch and enamoured swain.                      310
Led by my hand, he sauntered Europe round,
And gathered every vice on Christian ground;
Saw every court, heard every king declare
His royal sense of operas or the fair;
The stews and palace equally explored,                            315
Intrigued with glory, and with spirit whored;
Tried all hors-d'œuvres, all liqueurs defined,
Judicious drank, and greatly-daring dined;
Dropped the dull lumber of the Latin store,
Spoiled his own language, and acquired no more;                   320
All classic learning lost on classic ground;
And last turned air, the echo of a sound!
See now, half-cured, and perfectly well-bred,
With nothing but a solo in his head;
As much estate, and principle, and wit,                           325
As Jansen, Fleetwood, Cibber shall think fit;
Stolen from a duel, followed by a nun,
And, if a borough choose him, not undone;
See, to my country happy I restore
This glorious youth, and add one Venus more.                      330
Her, too, receive (for her my soul adores);
So may the sons of sons of sons of whores,
Prop thine, oh empress, like each neighbour throne,
And make a long posterity thy own.'
    Pleased, she accepts the hero and the dame,                   335
Wraps in her veil, and frees from sense of shame.
    Then looked, and saw a lazy, lolling sort,
Unseen at church, at senate, or at court,

Of ever-listless loiterers, that attend
No cause, no trust, no duty, and no friend.                    340
Thee too, my Paridel, she marked thee there,
Stretched on the rack of a too easy chair,
And heard thy everlasting yawn confess
The pains and penalties of idleness.
She pitied, but her pity only shed                             345
Benigner influence on thy nodding head.
    But Annius, crafty seer, with ebon wand,
And well dissembled emerald on his hand,
False as his gems, and cankered as his coins,
Came, crammed with capon, from where Pollio dines.            350
Soft, as the wily fox is seen to creep
Where bask on sunny banks the simple sheep,
Walk round and round, now prying here, now there;
So he; but pious, whispered first his prayer:
    'Grant, gracious goddess, grant me still to cheat –       355
Oh may thy cloud still cover the deceit!
Thy choicer mists on this assembly shed,
But pour them thickest on the noble head.
So shall each youth, assisted by our eyes,
See other Cæsars, other Homers rise;                          360
Through twilight ages hunt the Athenian fowl,
Which Chalcis gods, and mortals call an owl,
Now see an Atys, now a Cecrops clear,
Nay, Mahomet, the pigeon at thine ear,
Be rich in ancient brass, though not in gold,                 365
And keep his lares, though his house be sold;
To headless Phœbe his fair bride postpone,
Honour a Syrian prince above his own;
Lord of an Otho, if I vouch it true;
Blest in one Niger, till he knows of two.'                    370
    Mummius o'erheard him; Mummius, fool-renowned,
Who like his Cheops stinks above the ground,
Fierce as a startled adder, swelled, and said,
Rattling an ancient sistrum at his head:
    'Speakest thou of Syrian princes? Traitor base!           375
Mine, goddess, mine is all the horned race.
True, he had wit, to make their value rise;
From foolish Greeks to steal them, was as wise;

More glorious yet, from barbarous hands to keep,
When Sallee rovers chased him on the deep.                    380
Then taught by Hermes, and divinely bold,
Down his own throat he risked the Grecian gold;
Received each demigod, with pious care,
Deep in his entrails – I revered them there;
I bought them, shrouded in that living shrine                 385
And, at their second birth, they issue mine.'
    'Witness great Ammon, by whose horns I swore'
(Replied soft Annius) 'this our paunch before
Still bears them, faithful; and that thus I eat,
Is to refund the medals with the meat.                        390
To prove me, goddess, clear of all design,
Bid me with Pollio sup as well as dine:
There all the learned shall at the labour stand,
And Douglas lend his soft, obstetric hand.'
    The goddess, smiling, seemed to give consent;             395
So back to Pollio, hand in hand, they went.
    Then thick as locusts blackening all the ground,
A tribe, with weeds and shells fantastic crowned,
Each with some wondrous gift approached the power,
A nest, a toad, a fungus, or a flower.                        400
But far the foremost, two, with earnest zeal,
And aspect ardent to the throne appeal.
    The first thus opened: 'Hear thy suppliant's call,
Great queen, and common mother of us all!
Fair from its humble bed I reared this flower,                405
Suckled, and cheered, with air, and sun, and shower,
Soft on the paper ruff its leaves I spread,
Bright with the gilded button tipped its head,
Then throned in glass, and named it Caroline:
Each maid cried "charming", and each youth "divine":         410
Did Nature's pencil ever blend such rays,
Such varied light in one promiscuous blaze?
Now prostrate, dead, behold that Caroline:
No maid cries "charming", and no youth "divine" –
And lo the wretch, whose vile, whose insect, lust            415
Laid this gay daughter of the spring in dust.
Oh punish him, or to th' Elysian shades
Dismiss my soul, where no carnation fades.'

He ceased, and wept. With innocence of mien,
The accused stood forth, and thus addressed the queen:               420
    'Of all th' enamelled race, whose silvery wing
Waves to the tepid zephyrs of the spring,
Or swims along the fluid atmosphere,
Once brightest shined this child of heat and air.
I saw, and started from its vernal bower                             425
The rising game, and chased from flower to flower.
It fled, I followed; now in hope, now pain;
It stopped, I stopped; it moved, I moved again.
At last it fixed, 'twas on what plant it pleased,
And where it fixed, the beauteous bird I seized:                     430
Rose or carnation was below my care –
I meddle, goddess, only in my sphere.
I tell the naked fact without disguise,
And, to excuse it, need but show the prize;
Whose spoils this paper offers to your eye,                          435
Fair even in death, this peerless butterfly.'
    'My sons,' (she answered) 'both have done your parts:
Live happy both, and long promote our arts.
But hear a mother when she recommends
To your fraternal care our sleeping friends.                         440
The common soul, of heaven's more frugal make,
Serves but to keep fools pert, and knaves awake:
A drowsy watchman, that just gives a knock,
And breaks our rest, to tell us what's o'clock.
Yet by some object every brain is stirred;                           445
The dull may waken to a humming bird;
The most recluse, discreetly opened, find
Congenial matter in the cockle kind;
The mind, in metaphysics at a loss,
May wander in a wilderness of moss;                                  450
The head that turns at super-lunar things,
Poised with a tail, may steer on Wilkins' wings.
    Oh, would the sons of men once think their eyes
And reason given them but to study flies!
See Nature in some partial narrow shape,                             455
And let the author of the whole escape:
Learn but to trifle; or, who most observe,
To wonder at their maker, not to serve.'

'Be that my task' (replies a gloomy clerk,
Sworn foe to mystery, yet divinely dark;                          460
Whose pious hope aspires to see the day,
When moral evidence shall quite decay,
And damns implicit faith, and holy lies,
Prompt to impose, and fond to dogmatise):
'Let others creep by timid steps and slow,                        465
On plain experience lay foundations low,
By common sense to common knowledge bred,
And last, to Nature's cause through Nature led.
All-seeing in thy mists, we want no guide,
Mother of arrogance, and source of pride!                         470
We nobly take the high priori road,
And reason downward till we doubt of God:
Make Nature still encroach upon his plan,
And shove him off as far as ever we can:
Thrust some mechanic cause into his place,                        475
Or bind in matter, or diffuse in space.
Or, at one bound o'er-leaping all his laws,
Make God man's image, man the final cause,
Find virtue local, all relation scorn,
See all in self, and but for self be born:                        480
Of nought so certain as our reason still,
Of nought so doubtful as of soul and will.
Oh, hide the god still more, and make us see
Such as Lucretius drew, a god like thee:
Wrapped up in self, a god without a thought,                      485
Regardless of our merit or default.
Or that bright image to our fancy draw,
Which Theocles in raptured vision saw,
While through poetic scenes the genius roves,
Or wanders wild in academic groves;                               490
That Nature our society adores,
Where Tindal dictates, and Silenus snores.'
    Roused at his name, up rose the boozy sire,
And shook from out his pipe the seeds of fire;
Then snapped his box, and stroked his belly down:                 495
Rosy and reverend, though without a gown.
Bland and familiar to the throne he came,
Led up the youth, and called the goddess 'dame'.

Then thus: 'From priest-craft happily set free,
Lo, every finished son returns to thee:                              500
First slave to words, then vassal to a name,
Then dupe to party; child and man the same;
Bounded by Nature, narrowed still by Art,
A trifling head, and a contracted heart.
Thus bred, thus taught, how many have I seen,                        505
Smiling on all, and smiled on by a queen.
Marked out for honours, honoured for their birth,
To thee the most rebellious things on earth:
Now to thy gentle shadow all are shrunk,
All melted down, in pension, or in punk!                             510
So Kent, so Berkeley, sneaked into the grave,
A monarch's half, and half a harlot's slave.
Poor Warwick nipped in folly's broadest bloom,
Who praises now? – His chaplain on his tomb.
Then take them all, oh take them to thy breast:                      515
Thy magus, goddess, shall perform the rest.'
     With that, a wizard old his cup extends,
Which whoso tastes, forgets his former friends,
Sire, ancestors, himself. One casts his eyes
Up to a star, and like Endymion dies:                               520
A feather shooting from another's head
Extracts his brain, and principle is fled,
Lost is his God, his country, everything,
And nothing left but homage to a king!
The vulgar herd turn off to roll with hogs,                          525
To run with horses, or to hunt with dogs;
But, sad example, never to escape
Their infamy, still keep the human shape.
     But she, good goddess, sent to every child
Firm impudence, or stupefaction mild;                               530
And straight succeeded, leaving shame no room,
Cibberian forehead, or Cimmerian gloom.
     Kind Self-conceit to some her glass applies,
Which no one looks in with another's eyes:
But as the flatterer or dependant paint,                            535
Beholds himself a patriot, chief, or saint.
     On others Interest her gay livery flings –
Interest, that waves on parti-coloured wings:

Turned to the sun, she casts a thousand dyes,
And, as she turns, the colours fall or rise.                    540
    Others the siren sisters warble round,
And empty heads console with empty sound.
No more, alas, the voice of Fame they hear,
The balm of Dullness trickling in their ear.
Great Cowper, Harcourt, Parker, Raymond, King,           545
Why all your toils? Your sons have learned to sing.
How quick Ambition hastes to ridicule!
The sire is made a peer, the son a fool.
    On some, a priest succinct in amice white
Attends; all flesh is nothing in his sight!               550
Beeves at his touch at once to jelly turn,
And the huge boar is shrunk into an urn:
The board with specious miracles he loads,
Turns hares to larks, and pigeons into toads.
Another (for in all what one can shine?)                  555
Explains the *sève* and *verdeur* of the vine.
What cannot copious sacrifice attone?
Thy truffles, Perigord! Thy hams, Bayonne!
With French libation, and Italian strain,
Wash Bladen white, and expiate Hays's stain.             560
Knight lifts the head, for what are crowds undone
To three essential partridges in one?
Gone every blush, and silent all reproach,
Contending princes mount them in their coach.
    Next bidding all draw near on bended knees,           565
The queen confers her titles and degrees.
Her children first of more distinguished sort,
Who study Shakespeare at the Inns of Court,
Impale a glow-worm, or vertù profess,
Shine in the dignity of F. R. S.                          570
Some, deep freemasons, join the silent race,
Worthy to fill Pythagoras's place:
Some botanists, or florists at the least,
Or issue members of an annual feast.
Nor passed the meanest unregarded, one                    575
Rose a Gregorian, one a Gormogon.
The last, not least in honour or applause,
Isis and Cam made Doctors of her Laws.

   Then blessing all: 'Go, children of my care,
To practice now from theory repair.                          580
All my commands are easy, short, and full:
My sons, be proud, be selfish, and be dull!
Guard my prerogative, assert my throne:
This nod confirms each privilege your own.
The cap and switch be sacred to his grace;                   585
With staff and pumps the marquis lead the race;
From stage to stage the licensed earl may run,
Paired with his fellow-charioteer the sun;
The learned baron butterflies design,
Or draw to silk Arachne's subtle line;                       590
The judge to dance his brother serjeant call;
The senator at cricket urge the ball;
The bishop stow (pontific luxury!)
An hundred souls of turkeys in a pie;
The sturdy squire to Gallic masters stoop,                   595
And drown his lands and manors in a soup.
Others import yet nobler arts from France,
Teach kings to fiddle, and make senates dance.
Perhaps more high some daring son may soar,
Proud to my list to add one monarch more;                    600
And nobly conscious, princes are but things
Born for first ministers, as slaves for kings,
Tyrant supreme, shall three estates command,
And MAKE ONE MIGHTY DUNCIAD OF THE LAND!'
   More she had spoke, but yawned – all nature nods:        605
What mortal can resist the yawn of gods?
Churches and chapels instantly it reached;
(St James's first, for leaden Gilbert preached)
Then catched the schools; the Hall scarce kept awake;
The convocation gaped, but could not speak:                 610
Lost was the nation's sense, nor could be found,
While the long solemn unison went round:
Wide, and more wide, it spread o'er all the realm;
Even Palinurus nodded at the helm:
The vapour mild o'er each committee crept;                  615
Unfinished treaties in each office slept;
And chiefless armies dozed out the campaign;
And navies yawned for orders on the main.

Oh Muse, relate (for you can tell alone –
Wits have short memories, and dunces none),                    620
Relate who first, who last resigned to rest;
Whose heads she partly, whose completely blessed;
What charms could faction, what ambition lull,
The venal quiet, and entrance the dull;
'Till drowned was sense, and shame, and right, and wrong –   625
Oh sing, and hush the nations with thy song!

   *    *    *    *    *    *

In vain, in vain – the all-composing hour
Resistless falls: the Muse obeys the power.
She comes! She comes! The sable throne behold
Of Night primeval, and of Chaos old!                          630
Before her, Fancy's gilded clouds decay,
And all its varying rainbows die away.
Wit shoots in vain its momentary fires,
The meteor drops, and in a flash expires.
As one by one, at dread Medea's strain,                       635
The sickening stars fade off th'ethereal plain;
As Argus' eyes by Hermes' wand oppressed
Closed one by one to everlasting rest;
Thus at her felt approach, and secret might,
Art after art goes out, and all is night.                     640
See skulking Truth to her old cavern fled,
Mountains of casuistry heaped o'er her head!
Philosophy, that leaned on heaven before,
Shrinks to her second cause, and is no more.
Physic of Metaphysic begs defence,                            645
And Metaphysic calls for aid on Sense!
See Mystery to Mathematics fly!
In vain! They gaze, turn giddy, rave, and die.
Religion, blushing, veils her sacred fires,
And, unawares, Morality expires.                              650
Not public blame, nor private, dares to shine;
Nor human spark is left, nor glimpse divine!
Lo! thy dread empire, CHAOS, is restored;
Light dies before thy uncreating word.
Thy hand, great anarch, lets the curtain fall,                655
And universal darkness buries all.

# Notes

Except for *The Dunciad*, texts for the present edition follow *The Works of Alexander Pope, Esq.*, 9 vols, ed. William Warburton, 1751 (modernised).

## Abbreviations

*Met.*: = Ovid, *Metamorphoses*
[P]: a note (or information) by Pope himself.

**Windsor-Forest**: first published 1713. **Lansdowne**: George Granville, Baron Lansdowne (1667–1735), Tory and Jacobite; praised by Pope as a poet. He invited Pope to write this celebration of the Peace of Utrecht (1713). **1 Windsor**: Pope's family lived at Binfield, near Windsor. **7 Eden**: Genesis, ii–iii; Milton, *Paradise Lost*, Book 4. **14 harmoniously confused**: traditional description of the cosmos from Plato, *Timaeus*, on. **31 oaks . . . borne**: Virgil, *Eclogues*, 4.30; also, English ships. **33 Olympus**: home of the gods. **37 Pan**: tradnlly lustful half-goat, half-human, god of nature, shepherds, etc. **37 Pomona**: goddess of fruit. **38 Flora**: goddess of flowers. **39 Ceres**: goddess of corn. **42 STUART**: i.e., Queen Anne (reigned 1702–14). **43 Not . . . past**: the tyrannies of the Norman kings (starting with William I) are seen in part as anticipating the arrival of William III in 1688. The enclosing of the New Forest as a hunting ground symbolises the denial of subjects' liberties (*foris* = beyond [common law]). **61 Nimrod**: Genesis, x:8–10, the 'mighty hunter', supposedly the first tyrant. **101 tainted**: carrying the prey's scent. **106 Albion**: England. **119 Arcturus**: in constellation Boötes, its heliacal rising in mid-September was associated with storms. **142 Tyrian**: crimson. **143 volumes**: coils. **147 Cancer**: the sun enters Cancer on 22 June. **159 Arcadia**: traditional pastoral paradise. **160 huntress**: the virginal hunting goddess Diana, with her nymphs. **162 chaste a queen**: Elizabeth I; also Queen Anne. **166 Cynthus**: Diana's mountain birthplace on the isle of Delos. **170 buskined**: wearing knee boots; **traced**: stepped or danced across. **172 Lodona**: the Loddon flows into the Thames near

Binfield; Pope's metamorphic tale has sources in, among others, Ovid (*Met.*, 1.452ff.; 5.572ff.), Spenser (*Faerie Queene*, 2.2.7–9). **176 zone**: girdle. **178 fillet**: ribbon. **179 sounds**: proclaims (her status). **186 liquid**: bright. **200 Cynthia**: name for Diana (166n. above). **223 Neptune's self**: Neptune was the Roman god of the seas. **227–8 Po . . . strays**: the river Po was anciently identified with the constellation Eridanus. **233 Jove**: the king of the gods lusted after various mortals. **242 spoils**: strips. **243 exalts**: intensifies (alchemical). **244 draws**: breathes in. **257 Scipio**: Scipio Africanus (d. 183 BC), victor over Hannibal, withdrew to exile to his estate at Liternum. **258 Atticus . . . Trumbull**: Titus Pomponius (d. 32 BC) rejected politics and spent much of his life studying in Athens (hence Atticus); Sir William **Trumbull**: (d. 1716), distinguished politician and friend of Pope after his retirement to an estate near Binfield. **259 nine**: the Muses. **271 Denham**: Sir John (d. 1669); Pope refers to *Cooper's Hill* (1642; 1655). **272 Cowley**: Abraham, the poet (d. 1667, near Windsor). **290 star**: emblem of the Order of the Garter. **291 Surrey**: Henry Howard, Earl of Surrey (d. 1547) addressed poems to the Lady Elizabeth Fitzgerald as Geraldine. **303 Edward**: Edward III. **305 Cressy**: Edward III was victorious over the French at Cressy (1346). **307 Verrio's colours**: Antonio Verrio (d. 1707) painted decorative ceilings, etc. **311 Henry**: Henry VI. **313 martyr-king**: Charles I. **314 Edward**: Edward IV. **316 Bellerium**: Land's End. **323 purple deaths**: the Plague (1665). **324 fire**: of London (1666). **336 Augusta**: Roman name for London. **345 Vandalis**: the river Wandle. **368 Iber . . . Ister**: the Ebro; the Danube. **381 There . . . doom**: echoing, up to 422, Isaiah, lx. **387 cross**: the red cross of St George. **396 Phœbus**: the sun (the ripening idea was commonplace). **419 Envy**: a snake was her emblem. **422 Furies**: goddesses of vengeance. **429 Peace**: her emblems are the olive and dove. **434 sylvan strains**: Pope recalls line 1 of his pastoral 'Spring', because Virgil closed the *Georgics* with the opening of his *Eclogues*.

**The Rape of the Lock**: first published 1712; enlarged 1714. CANTO 1 **3 Caryll**: John (d. 1736), friend of Pope, had suggested that Pope write the poem to reconcile the respective families after Robert, Lord Petre, had cut off a lock of Arabella Fermor's hair. **9 unexplored**: undiscovered. **13 Sol**: the sun. **20 sylph**: Pope explains in his dedicatory letter that the quasi-epic supernatural machinery of elemental spirits derives from the amusing pseudo-Rosicrucian *Le Comte de Gabalis* (*Cabbalistic Count*) by the Abbé de Montfaucon de Villars (1670; English trans., 1680). **23 birth-night**:

royal birthday celebrations. Such divine apparitions are common-place (e.g., Mercury to Aeneas in *Aeneid* 4), but Pope also recalls Satan to Eve in Milton, *Paradise Lost* 4.800. **44 Ring**: small ballustraded, elevated round area in Hyde Park used for leisure drives. **45 equipage**: coach, horses and attendants. **46 chair**: sedan chair. **56 ombre**: 3. 27n. below. **59 termagant**: a quarrelsome woman. **73 spark**: showy youth (contemptuous). **85 stars**: *WF*, 290n. **89 blush to know**: with rouge. **101 sword-knots**: decorative ribbons attached to sword-hilt. **106 Ariel**: elemental spirit in Shakespeare's *Tempest*, but found in various occult sources. **115 Shock**: (or shough) – fashionable shaggy, curly-coated lap-dogs. **131 nicely**: delicately. **139 awful**: terrifying, awe-inspiring. **148 Betty**: traditional name for lady's maid. CANTO 2 **27 tresses ... ensnare**: a commonplace: e.g., Spenser, *Amoretti*, 37. **35 Phœbus**: *WF*, 396n. **47 But ... glides**: cf. Cleopatra on the Cydnus (Shakespeare, *Antony and Cleopatra*, II.2). **64 filmy dew**: gos-samer. **71 purple**: brilliant. **74 genii**: guardian angels. **82 stars ... night**: shooting stars. **84 painted bow**: rainbow. **100 furbe-low**: pleated border of gown. **104 the Fates**: Clotho (draws the thread of life into existence); Lachesis (controls the thread during lifetime); Atropos (cuts the thread at death: cf. the cutting of Belinda's lock). **113 drops**: diamond earrings. **129 pomatums**: i.e., pomade (scented ointment, often for the head). **132 rivelled**: shrivelled. **133 Ixion**: tied to a wheel in hell for attempting to violate Juno, queen of heaven. CANTO 3 **4 Hampton**: Hampton Court. **7 three realms**: Britain, Ireland, France. **27 ombre**: fashionable card game, named after Spanish *hombre* (man), but suggesting also French *ombre* (shade). **33 matador**: principal cards in ombre. **49 Spadillio**: ace of spades. **51 Manillio**: second best trump (2 of clubs or spades; 7 of diamonds or hearts). **53 Basto**: ace of clubs. **61 Pam**: knave of clubs (highest trump in the game 5-card loo). **67 Amazon**: ancient race of militant women. **92 codille**: term used in ombre for the losing of game by player challenging to win. **107 altars of japan**: fashionable japanned (laquered) tables. **122 Scylla's fate**: *Met.*, 8.1ff.; she cut a sacred hair from her father, Nisus's, head, to guarantee victory in battle to his enemy, Minos. As a punishment she was turned into a bird, Ciris (from Greek *keiro* = I cut). **147 forfex**: pair of scissors (Latin). **165 Atalantis**: Delarivière Manley's satirical *Secret Memoirs and Manners of several Persons of Quality, of both Sexes. From the new Atalantis* (1709). CANTO 4 **1 But ... oppressed**: echoes *Aeneid*, 4.1. **8 manteau**: loose upper garment (mantle). **16 Spleen**: fashionable hypochondriac melancholy (the 'vapours'). Umbriel's journey parallels

Aeneas's descent to the underworld holding the golden bough (*Aeneid*, 6).
**24 Megrim**: Migraine. **51 pipkin ... walks**: pipkin: small earthen-
ware cook-pot; for the Homer, see *Iliad*, 18.439ff. **60 poetic fit**: it was
common to distinguish between physical and inspirational melancholy.
**69 citron-waters**: brandy flavoured with lemon peel. **82 Ulysses ...
winds**: Homer, *Odyssey*, 10.19ff. **89 Thalestris**: named after the queen
of the Amazons (3. 67n.). **101 fillets**: *WF*, 178n. **117 Circus**: the
Ring (1.44n.). **124 clouded**: veined. **156 bohea**: finest quality tea.
CANTO 5 **5 Trojan**: Aeneas at *Aeneid*, 4.296ff. **37 virago**: female
warrior. **40 whalebones**: giving structure to the petticoats. **47 Pallas
... arms**: Pallas (or Athene), militant virginal goddess of wisdom; **Mars**:
god of war; **Latona**: the mother of Apollo and Diana; despised by Niobe,
she caused her children to kill Niobe's family; **Hermes**: (Mercury)
messenger of the gods among other functions. **50 Neptune**: *WF*, 223n.
**65 Meander**: winding river in Phrygia. **71 golden scales**: the scales of
justice; cf. *Aeneid*, 12.725ff; *Paradise Lost*, 4.997ff. (which has *golden scales*).
The battle is full of echoes of the *Iliad* and *Aeneid*. **89 The same**: the
bodkin's history imitates that of Agamemnon's sceptre at *Iliad*, 2.129ff.
**105 Othello**: Shakespeare, *Othello*, IV.1. **113 lunar sphere**: repository
of lost things in Ariosto, *Orlando Furioso* 34.73ff. **126 Proculus**: reputedly
had a vision of the dead Romulus, 'Rome's great founder' (125), telling him
that he should be worshipped as the god Quirinus (Ovid, *Fasti*, 2.499ff.).
**129 Berenice's lock**: Berenice, wife of Ptolemy Euergetes, dedicated a
lock of hair for her husband's safe return from Syria. It was reputedly turned
into a constellation: Catullus, *Carmina*, 66, locates it in Venus' bosom.
**133 the Mall**: enclosed walk built by Charles II in St James's Park, it
became a fashionable resort. **136 Rosamonda's lake**: pond in St James's
Park. **137 Partridge**: John, the astrologer (d. 1715): 'a ridiculous star-
gazer, who in his almanacs every year never failed to predict the downfall of
the pope, and the king of France [Louis XIV], then at war with the English'
[P]. **138 Galileo's eyes**: the telescope, much improved by Galileo (d.
1642).

*Eloisa to Abelard*: first published 1717. An imitation of Ovid's heroic
epistles (*Heroides*: monologues uttered by a woman abandoned by her
lover). The story of the scholar-teacher Abelard's seduction of the learned
young girl, Heloïse, was one of the most famous of the middle ages. He made
her pregnant; they married secretly, with Heloïse publicly denying the
marriage. She then went to a monastery (later becoming a nun), while
Abelard, castrated by Heloïse's relatives (who believed that he had let her
down over the marriage), became a monk, later founding the Convent of the

Paraclete (the Holy Spirit as aid and comforter) and subsequently, while he was an abbot in Brittany, putting Heloïse in charge. He died in 1142, condemned for his teachings, and was buried at the Paraclete. Heloïse died in 1164 and was buried with him. Their letters were published in Latin in 1616; Pope used the English prose translation by John Hughes (1713) closely, with additional indebtedness to the pre-Puritan Milton of *Il Penseroso*, which inspired Pope to turn the traditional gloomy landscape of the forsaken lover into one of the earliest 'gothic' settings. **1 awful**: inspiring reverential fear. **2 Contemplation**: linked with Melancholy (cf. *RL*, 4.60n.) as in Dürer's *Melencolia 1* engraving (part of a long tradition). For the landscape and contemplative melancholy, see Milton's *Il Penseroso*. **4 vestal's**: i.e., virgin's (but Vesta was Roman goddess of the hearth, so Eloisa refers to the flames of love as well). **12 idea**: image. **20 shagged**: rough. **24 I ... stone**: *Il Penseroso*, 42. **38 convent**: i.e., monastery. **62 Mind**: i.e., God as Intellect. **63 attempering**: moderating. **64 lambent**: softly radiant. **100 bleeding**: refers to his castration. **134 paradise ... wild**: reversing Genesis, iii, where man is expelled from Eden into the wilderness after the Fall. **144 dim...light**: 'windows richly dight,/Casting a dim religious light' (*Il Penseroso*, 159–60). **150 charity**: [Christian] love (Latin *caritas*). **162 visionary**: seeing visions. **165 Melancholy**: Greek for 'black bile' (its supposed physical cause). **170 browner**: gloomier; **horror**: terrifying ruggedness. **177 spouse of God**: nuns take marriage vows to Christ. **202 raped**: possessed by divine ecstasy. **212 Obedient ... weep**: Richard Crashaw, 'Description of a Religious House' 16. **220 hymeneals**: marriage songs. **249 Fates**: *RL*, 2.104n.

***Elegy to the Memory of an Unfortunate Lady***: first published 1717. While caring for Mrs Elizabeth Weston and Mrs Ann Cope (both separated from their husbands), and suffering from the absence of Lady Mary Wortley Montagu in eastern Europe and Turkey, Pope wrote this purely fictional elegiac modulation of the heroic epistle. **8 Roman's part**: suicide (the lady killed herself with a sword). **9 reversion**: inheritance. **41 Furies**: *WF*, 422n. **52 decent**: comely. **59 Loves**: Cupids. **66 blow**: bloom.

***Epistle to Burlington***: first published 1731. A Horatian epistle or 'moral essay' on false taste. **Burlington**: Richard Boyle, 3rd Earl of Burlington (1695–1753); friend of Pope and ardent advocate of the simple harmonies and symmetries of Palladian architecture. **7–10 Topham ... Sloane**:

Richard **Topham** (d. 1735); Thomas Herbert, 8th Earl of **Pembroke** (d. 1733); Thomas **Hearne** (d. 1735); Dr Richard **Mead** (d. 1754); Sir Hans **Sloane** (d. 1753). **13 Virro**: 'eminent man' (Italian). **15 Visto**: gaudy (Italian). **18 Ripley**: Thomas (d. 1758), architect. **30 arcs**: arches. **34 rustic**: rough finish. **36 Venetian door**: door or window in Palladian style. **46 Jones . . . Le Nôtre**: the Palladian, Inigo **Jones** (d. 1652); the French formal garden designer Andre **Le Nôtre** (d. 1700). **57 genius**: the *genius loci* (guardian spirit of the place) – its 'feel'. **70 Stowe**: the gardens were designed by Charles Bridgeman, William Kent and others. Richard Temple, Viscount Cobham (d. 1749) lived there. **78 Dr Clarke**: Samuel (d. 1729), whose bust was placed in the Hermitage in Richmond Park. **79 Villario**: 'owner of a country seat/park' (Italian). **89 Sabinus**: Sabinus Tyro wrote an ancient treatise on gardening. **95 flourished**: covered in flowers. **99 Timon**: pride, aristocratic false honour (Greek *timē*). **104 Brobdignag**: land of giants in Swift, *Gulliver's Travels*, 2. **123 Amphitrite**: wife of Neptune (*WF*, 223n.). **136 Aldus**: Aldo Manutio, early Renaissance Venetian printer; the Abbé Du Seuil was a celebrated early 18th-century Paris bookbinder. **139 Locke**: John (d. 1704), philosopher. **146 Verrio**: *WF*, 307n.; Louis **Laguerre** (1663–1721) collaborated with Verrio on his arrival in England. **160 Sancho . . . wand**: Cervantes, *Don Quixote*, 2.47. **176 Ceres**: *WF*, 39n. **178 Bathurst**: Allen, Baron Bathurst (1685–1775), friend of Pope, dedicatee of Pope's *Epistle to Bathurst* (1733); **Boyle**: i.e., Burlington. **191 falling arts**: the London churches, built by order of Queen Anne, 'were ready to fall, being founded in boggy land' [P]. **194 Vitruvius**: M. Vitruvius Pollio, whose *Ten Books Concerning Architecture* (written 20–11 BC) was dedicated to the Emperor Augustus; deeply influential on Palladio and Jones (46n. above), his work inspired a Vitruvian (really neo-Palladian) revival in the early 18th century. **195 ideas** : concepts; archetypal patterns.

***Epistle to Dr Arbuthnot***: first published 1735, an Horatian epistle. **Arbuthnot**: Dr John Arbuthnot (1667–1735), Physician Extraordinary to Queen Anne, political satirist and mathematician, was a great friend of Pope. **3 dog-star**: Sirius, the heliacal rising of which in mid-July ushers in the dog-days, associated with madness (Bedlam, the London madhouse), pestilence and, in ancient Rome, the public rehearsing of poetry (Parnassus, home of the Muses). **8 grot**: Pope's underground grotto at Twickenham ('Twitnam'). **13 Mint**: refuge in Southwark for debtors. **23 Arthur**: Moore, economist; **son**: of Arthur, James Moore Smythe (d. 1734) is in *The Dunciad*. **40 Keep . . . years**: Horace, *Art of Poetry*, 388.

**41 high ... Lane**: in a garret in a well-known disreputable area.
**49 Pitholeon**: 'the name taken from a foolish poet at Rhodes' [P].
**53 Curll**: Edmund (d. 1747), infamous bookseller; a main target in *The Dunciad*. **62 Lintot**: Barnaby Bernard (d. 1736); published Pope's *Homer*, but again in *The Dunciad*. **66 go snacks**: share the proceeds. **69 Midas'** ... **spring**: *Met.*, 11.146ff. (preferring the music of Pan to that of Apollo, Midas is given ass's ears; in Ovid, his barber can't keep the secret; according to Chaucer's 'Wife of Bath's Tale' (tr. Dryden, *Fables* 185ff.), it is the queen).
**80 ass**: the ass, emblem of stupidity, appeared on the title-page to the 1729 *Dunciad Variorum*. **85 Codrus**: poet ridiculed for vanity by Virgil.
**96 Parnassian sneer**: phrase applied to critic and writer Lewis Theobald (d. 1744) as hero of 1729 *Dunciad*, 2.5. **97 Colley**: Cibber (d. 1757), dramatist, theatre manager, poet laureate from 1730; hero of the 1743 *Dunciad*. **98 Henley**: 'Orator' John Henley (d. 1756); worked for Robert Walpole and Curll (53n.); as an itinerant preacher he had delivered a sermon on the butchering trade (1729); **Moore**: James Moore Smythe (23n.) was a freemason, an institution much satirised at the time.
**99 Bavius**: vituperated enemy of Virgil and Horace. **100 Philips**: Ambrose (d. 1749), rival to Pope as pastoral poet, secretary to Hugh Boulter, Archbishop of Armagh. **101 Sappho**: sixth-century BC lyric poetess of Lesbos. **111 Grub Street**: home of hack writers, situated on the present Barbican site. **117 Ammon's ... son**: Alexander the Great, who claimed descent from Jupiter Ammon. **118 Ovid's nose**: alluding to the poet's family name, Ovidius Naso. Latin *nasus* (nose). **122 Maro**: the Roman epic poet, Virgilius Maro. **135 Granville**: *WF*, title n.
**136 Walsh**: William (d. 1708), wit, politician, poet and early friend of Pope. **137 Garth**: Dr Samuel (d. 1719), poet and physician; another early friend of Pope. **138 Congreve**: William (d. 1729), dramatist and poet; **Swift**: Jonathan (d. 1745), satirist, poet and divine, was a close friend of Pope. **139 Talbot**: Charles, Earl and first Duke of Shrewsbury; **Somers**, Sir John, Lord; **Sheffield**: John, Duke of Buckingham, both patrons and politicians. **140 Rochester**: Francis Atterbury (d. 1732), Bishop of Rochester, Jacobite friend of Pope. **141 St John's self**: Henry St John, Viscount Bolingbroke (d. 1751), Tory politician, monarchical theorist and friend of Pope. **146 Burnet**: Sir Thomas (d. 1753), attacked Pope's Homer; **Old mixon**: John (d. 1742), associated with Curll, also attacked Pope; **Cook**: Thomas (d. 1756), a Curll author and enemy of Pope. All are in *The Dunciad*. **151 Gildon**: Charles (d. 1724), dramatist and enemy of Pope. **153 Dennis**: John (d. 1734), critic, dramatist and target of Pope.
**164 Bentley**: Richard (d. 1742), scholar; master of Trinity College,

Cambridge; target of Pope and others, here attacked for his emendations to *Paradise Lost* (1732); **Tibbald**: 96n. **180 Persian tale**: trans. by Philips (100n.). **190 Tate**: Nahum (d. 1715), librettist; gave *King Lear* a happy ending. **192 Addison**: Joseph (d. 1719), politician, poet, critic and essayist; edited *The Spectator* with Sir Richard Steele; Pope had an uneasy relationship with him. **209 Cato**: M. Porcius Cato Censorius (d. 149 BC), regarded for military excellence and as an embodiment of ideal Roman virtue; the subject of Addison's *Cato* (1713); this line quotes Pope's 'Prologue' to *Cato*, 23. **211 templars**: lawyers. **214 Atticus**: WF, 258n.; he was a great friend of Cicero. Here he = Addison. **216 claps**: posters (Pope refers to book title-pages being used as fly posters). **222 George . . . song**: the annual birthday odes for George II. **230 Bufo**: toad (Latin). Based in part on George Bubb Dodington (d. 1762), politician, patron and collector; **Castalian**: fountain Castalius at foot of Parnassus (3n.). **231 Apollo**: sun god; god of poetry and music. **236 Pindar**: 5th-century BC lyric poet. **248 bury . . . starve**: the poet and dramatist John Dryden (1631–1700) 'after having lived in exigencies, had a magnificent funeral bestowed upon him' [P]. **256 Gay**: Pope's friend John Gay (1685–1732), dramatist and poet. The Duke and Duchess of **Queensberry** (260) aided him in his last years and erected his monument in Westminster Abbey. **262 To . . . do**: Denham, *Of Prudence*, 93–4. **276 Balbus**: the opportunist Balbus who knew Cicero and was promoted by Augustus. **280 Sir Will**: Sir William Yonge, tool of Robert Walpole (prime minister until 1742); **Bubo**: (Latin = owl); i.e., Dodington (230n.). **300 Canons**: the splendid Middlesex house, built 1716–20 for James Brydges, first Duke of Chandos (d. 1744). **305 Sporus**: Nero's favourite youth, whom he had castrated and then married (Suetonius, *Nero*, 28.1); Pope means the effeminate John, Lord Hervey, Baron Ickworth (d. 1743), favourite of Queen Caroline; he used cosmetics to disguise his epileptic pallor. **314 mumbling**: chew toothlessly. **319 ear of Eve**: see *RL*, 1.23n. **330 Eve's tempter**: the tradition of the serpent at the Fall (Genesis, iii) having a female face has a long history in the visual arts. **353 pictured shape**: Pope as hunchbacked ape; frontispiece to *Pope Alexander's Supremacy* (1729), attack on 1729 *Dunciad*. **355 father, dead**: Alexander Pope senior died in 1717. **363 Japhet**: Japhet Crook (d. 1734), forger. **375 Welsted**: Leonard (d. 1747), who 'had the impudence to tell in print that Mr P had occasioned a lady's death [and] that he had libelled the Duke of Chandos' [P]. **378 Budgell**: Eustace (d. 1749), poet. **391 Bestia**: L. Calpurnius Bestia, Roman consul, 111 BC, known for his greed. Pope means the Duke of Marlborough (d. 1722).

**Epistle to a Lady**: first published 1735. Horatian epistle on traditional theme of female vanity and inconstancy; included later as no. 2 of the 4 moral essays of which Burlington was no.4. **Lady**: Pope's good friend (perhaps mistress) and early neighbour Martha Blount (1690–1763). **10 swan**: form in which Jove raped Leda. **12 Magdalene**: St Mary Magdalene, penitent whore. **13 Cecilia**: St Cecilia, virgin saint of music. **20 Cynthia**: moon (emblem of fickle change). **21 Rufa**: red-head (Latin). **24 Sappho**: (*Ep.Arb.*, 101n.) = Lady Mary (*Elegy ... Lady*, headnote). **29 Silia**: silent one (Latin). **31 Calista**: heroine of Thomas Rowe's tragedy *The Fair Penitent* (1703). **37 Papillia**: butterfly (Latin). **45 Calypso**: seduces Odysseus (*Odyssey*, 5). **53 Narcissa**: self-lover. **63 Taylor**: Jeremy, *Holy Living* (1650) and *Holy Dying* (1651); **Book of Martyrs**: popular name of John Foxe's protestant martyrology *Acts and Monuments* (1563). **64 citron**: *RL*, 4. 69n.; **Chartres**: Francis, cheat and rapist (d. 1731). **78 Tallboy**: simple lover in Richard Brome's *The Jovial Crew* (1641); **Charles**: generic for footman. **79 Helluo**: Glutton (Latin). **80 haut-gout**: food with strong scent or taste. **83 Philomede**: lover of bribes. **87 Flavia**: blonde (Latin). **101 Simo**: snub-nose (Greek); ape. **110 ratafie**: ratafia, fruit liqueur. **115 Atossa**: ambitious daughter of Cyrus the Great of Persia; based on Katherine, Duchess of Buckinghamshire (d. 1743) and perhaps Sarah, Duchess of Marlborough (d. 1744). **157 Chloe**: common name in pastoral love poetry. **182 queen**: Caroline, disliked by Pope for her politics. **193 Queensberry**: *Ep. Arb.*, 256n. **194 Helen**: of Troy. **198 Mahomet**: Turkish servant of George I; **Hale**: Stephen Hales (d. 1761), curate of Teddington, Middx. **251 Ring**: *RL*, 1.44n. **266 codille**: *RL*, 3.92n. **283 Phœbus**: the sun god; see *WF*, 396n.

*The Dunciad*: text: *The Dunciad, in Four Books* (1743; modernised). First published 1728 (3 books); rev. 1729 as *The Dunciad Variorum* with copious notes; *The New Dunciad* (1742) was the first publication of what in 1743, expanded, would be Book 4. In 1743 Cibber (*Ep. Arb.*, 97n.) displaces Lewis Theobald (*Ep. Arb.*, 96n.) as hero. Pope's mini-epic attack on contemporary culture recalls the *Aeneid*, *Paradise Lost* and Dryden's satirical squib on rival dramatist Thomas Shadwell, *MacFlecknoe* (1682). Given its formidable wealth of detail, the poem can be annotated only lightly here. BOOK 1 traces the origin of Dullness, changes scene to a London Lord Mayor's day (the city represents for Pope the uncultured Whig mercantile interest), and shows Dullness crowning Cibber as her laureate. BOOK 4 shows Dullness possessing all the arts and sciences, and ends with an apocalyptic vision of her coming. Pope's own notes are omitted for reasons of space. BOOK 1 **4 Jove**: king of heaven. **6 Dunce**: King George. **10 Pallas**: goddess of wisdom. **20 Dean ... Gulliver**: i.e. Jonathan Swift: *Ep. Arb.*, 138n. **22 Rabelais**: François (d. 1553), French comic writer. **28 Saturnian**: Saturn ruled the ideal, *golden*, first age of the world (but in alchemy, Saturn = lead [P]). **37 Proteus**: tricky, shape-changing sea god. **40 Curll ... Lintot**: *Ep. Arb.*, 53, 62, 216nn. **44 Grub Street**: *Ep. Arb.*, 111n. **46 virtues**: the 4 classical moral virtues. **57 Jacob**: Giles (d. 1744), law-writer; **warm**: rich; **third day**: author's benefit night. **86 Cimon**: Athenian general; Pope refers to the Lord Mayor of London's inaugural procession in October. **90 Settle**: Elkanah (d. 1724), mayoral pageant writer. **103 Daniel**: Defoe, pilloried like William Prynne (d. 1669). **104 Eusden**: Laurence (d. 1730), poet laureate; **Blackmore**: Sir Richard (d. 1729), poet. **105-6 Philips ... Dennis**: *Ep. Arb.*, 100, 153, 190nn. **108 Bays**: cf. poet laureate's laurel crown (refs to mainly 17th-century writers follow). **149 Wynkyn**: de Worde, succeeded printer William **Caxton** (d. 1491). **168 butt**: barrel of sack (laureate's perk). **208 Ridpath**: George (d. 1726), Whig journalist; **Mist**: Nathaniel (d. 1737), Tory publisher. **211 geese**: *Aeneid*, 8.655-6. **250 Perolla**: play by Cibber (1705). **255 Priam**: Aeneas's father, at Troy's destruction (*Aeneid*, 2). **270 quidnuncs**: gossips. **290 Heidegger**: John (d. 1749), Swiss impresario and master of the revels. **323 Needham's**: bawdy house. **330 King Log**: the fable of the frogs choosing a king in John Ogilby, *The Fables of Aesop Paraphrased in Verse* (1668 edn), fable 12. BOOK 4 **9 dogstar**: *Ep. Arb.*, 3n. **10 bay**: Book 1, 108n. **11 owl**: emblem of darkness but also wisdom. **16 lead**: Book 1, 28n. **29 straiten**: tighten. **31 Mathesis**: Mathematics. **41 Thalia**: Muse of comedy. **43 Chesterfield**: Philip Dormer Stanhope, 4th Earl of (d. 1773), opposed the 1737 Licensing Act submitting drama to a censor. **45 harlot**: 'Italian opera; its affected airs, its effeminate sounds [i.e., castrato singers] ...' [P]. **61 Phœbus**: i.e., Apollo (*Ep. Arb.*, 231n.). **65 Handel**: George Frederick (d. 1759); celebrated for his Italian operas, but then fell out of favour. His *Messiah* had a triumph in Dublin (1742). **66 Briareus**: ancient rebellious giant. **93 Baal**: biblical false god. **107 Patriots**: the opposition to Walpole's (*Ep. Arb.*, 280n.) Whig administration, the *Courtiers*. **110 Benson**: William (d. 1754), erected monument to **Milton** (112) and commissioned bust of poet Arthur **Johnston** (d. 1641) (112). **121 Medea**: *Met.*,

7.164ff. **144 Winton**: Winchester (Pope refers to Dr Busby, famous flogging head of Westminster). **151 Samian letter**: Y as Pythagorean emblem. **176 James**: the scholarly James I (d. 1625). **196 Locke**: *Ep. Burl.*, 139n. **198 Crousaz**: Jean (d. 1748), philosopher. **198 Burgers-dyck**: Francis (d. 1629), philosopher. **201 Bentley**: *Ep. Arb.*, 164n. **203 Aristarch**: commentator on Homer [P]. **245 Barrow**: Isaac (d. 1677), Master of Trinity, Cambridge. **246 Atterbury**: *Ep. Arb.*, 140n. **347 Annius**: mediaeval forger. **362 owl**: 11n. above. **371 Mummius**: 2nd-century BC Roman general; pillaged Greek art (here probably Dr Mead: *Ep. Burl.*, 7–10n.). **374 sistrum**: tambourine. **484 Lucretius**: *De rerum natura* (tr. Creech, 1699), 1.77ff. **488 Theocles**: Shaftesbury, 'The Moralists: A Philosophical Rhapsody' (1709). **492 Silenus**: satyr wine-god (Virgil, *Eclogue*, 6). **516 magus**: i.e., Robert Walpole (107n.). **520 Endymion**: beloved of moon goddess, who put him to eternal sleep. **532 Cimmerian**: underworld. **570 F. R. S.**: Fellow of the Royal Society. **572 Pythagoras's place**: Pythagoreans took a vow of silence. **590 Arachne**: turned into a spider (*Met.*, 6.1ff.). **635 Medea**: Seneca, *Medea*, Act 4. **637 Argus**: *Met.*, 1.682ff.